Endorse

"What a gift! *Live Your Life of Abundance* demystifies tried and true principles for life and money into simple and doable actions. Margo has beautifully written a resource that's as fun and easy to read as it is useful."
—Josh Spurlock, Founder @ MyCounselor.Online

"Margo Spidle's, *Live Your Life of Abundance*, is an authentic labor of love encouraging us to grasp our divine calling to live our life through the lens of love, gratitude, peace, and abundance while exhorting others. Our Creator equipped us with unique gifts, talents, and abilities to serve others along our human journey. I have known Margo for several years and I am blessed to call her a friend. She illuminates a true servant leader's heart demonstrating integrity, humility, and generosity in her calling."
— Terry M. Muns, Managing Director,
MLG Capital Group, LLC

Margo Spilde walks us through detailed yet simple to execute exercises to help the reader to not only identify what is uniquely important to them but also gives specific steps on how to implement each section so that they too can live a life of abundance. Reading this book makes me want to schedule a private retreat to spend time intentionally thinking about what it means to live a life of abundance and begin to implement her step-by-step action plan immediately. This is a book that can change the direction of your life if you give it a chance.
—Gretchen Cliburn, CFP®

"If the idea of planning for the next thirty years seems daunting or overwhelming, then this book is for you. Spilde breaks down an easy-to-follow process that creates time and space for you to dream big while also creating tangible steps to help you realize those dreams."

—Logan Aguirre, Publisher, *417 Magazine*

LIVE
your
LIFE
of
ABUNDANCE

MARGO SPILDE

Published by Freiling Publishing, a division of Freiling Agency, LLC.

P.O. Box 1264
Warrenton, VA 20188

www.FreilingPublishing.com

PB ISBN: 978-1-956267-49-5
e-Book ISBN: 978-1-956267-51-8

Printed in the United States of America

You were born with Potential.
You were born with Goodness and Trust.
You were born with Ideals and Dreams.
You were born with Greatness.
You were born with Wings.
You were not meant for crawling, so don't.
You have wings. Learn to use them and Fly.

by Jelaluddin Rumi

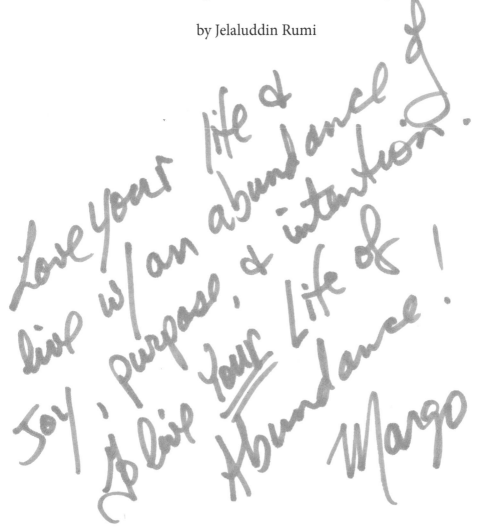

Love your life & live w/ an abundance of Joy, purpose, & intention. To live your life of Abundance!

Margo

Gratitude

I WANT TO say a special thank you to the people who continue to bring the most meaning and impact to my life. These people loved me when I did not feel lovable. Thank you for caring for me and standing by my side.

My husband Troy, you have never doubted me, and you continue to say yes to every ridiculous idea that pops in my head. I'm thankful for your willingness not to question or doubt my ideas and decisions. Your support is steadfast, and I appreciate how you always come along with me in any direction I decide to go. Thank you for encouraging me and joining me on this journey of life.

To our kids, Kirsten, Bret, and Alexa. You are kind, loving, and talented people. Each of you has special gifts and impact to leave on the people around you. Thank you for going along with all my crazy ideas, for traveling and finding adventure with me, and most of all, for allowing me the space and time to follow my passions and purpose. I'm excited to find out what amazing things you do in this world.

To the amazing and powerful women who I have the privilege to call friends. Thank you for standing beside me and loving me:

Christen Jeschke—Thank you for listening, trusting, and believing in me. Thank you for always encouraging me and blessing me with your strength. You were my friend before I felt worthy of having a friend, and that is a gift I can never repay. You are a blessing in my life, and I adore you. Without you, I would not have moved into my purpose. Your friendship is invaluable and God-inspired.

Aimee Dixon Plumlee—Thank you for traveling halfway around the world to become my friend. You are a blessing in my life, and I enjoy our real estate connection and conversations.

Thank you for offering to help with this book. Your editing skills are incredibly impressive. You have turned this book into a useful, understandable, and enjoyable tool that we can share with the world. Thank you for investing your time to bring this message forward. I'm excited to see what we can do next.

Gretchen Cliburn—You have given me the courage to do things that I would never have taken on myself. Without you, I would still be having meetings and not doing. Thank you for bringing your organizational skills, planning ahead, and creating structure to a vision worth sharing with the world. You are a beautiful soul, and I am excited for all the women of worth whose lives you are changing.

Rhonda Kelly—You are a kind and loving soul. Thank you for encouraging me and giving me the strength to stand up and be seen. Your gifts are a blessing to this world. Thank you for sharing them with me. You are a true gift to everyone around you.

Denine Bischoff—Thank you for reaching out to me and starting a beautiful friendship. When you stand beside me, I feel encouraged and confident. Thank you for believing in and investing in me. You are thoughtful, joyful, motivated, and smart. It is a blessing to know you and see all the lives you impact.

Tiffany Gish—Your joy and enthusiasm are a gift to everyone, especially me. Thank you for always being the other expressive, loud real estate woman in this town. You are a blessing, and I am grateful for your can-do attitude and am forever thankful for the opportunity to know you. This journey is just getting started. Lipstick and a seat belt are all that are needed on this thrilling ride.

To my real estate guy friends, Randy Swartzentruber, James McDonald, Daniel Brown, and Dave Aguirre—You mean the world to me. Thank you for believing in me and my ability to do real estate well. Your collaboration, experience, questions, courage, and confidence are a blessing to me, and I value you more than you can imagine. I would not be the person I am today without your friendship. Thank you for all you have done to invest in me and for your continued insight, friendship, and camaraderie.

Special thanks to Josh Spurlock, who knows more about me than anyone on the planet and still enjoys me. Thank you for helping me find my voice and discover my purpose. Your encouragement has helped me move forward despite the fear and learn how to not let setbacks discourage me. Without you, none of these relationships would be meaningful or possible, and nobody would ever hear what I have to share. The time you invested in me has been a huge blessing. Thank you for sitting with me, listening to me, looking at me, and sharing yourself with me. You have given me the courage and strength to stand up, show up, speak up, and be seen in this world. You have made the biggest impact on my life, and I am forever grateful for you. You are blessed to be a blessing.

Table of Contents

Prelude

/ˈprel͜(y)o͞od/

noun

An action or event serving as an introduction to
something more important.

MY PURPOSE IS to equip others to be who God has called them
to be. My goal in writing this book is to equip you to become the
person you are destined to become. Being equipped means you
are transformed from the inside. There are two attitudes you will
need to become functionally capable of being equipped. The first
is to be *receptive* to becoming changed and *aware* of where you
are in the present. The second is to be willing to be transformed
and *open* to becoming a new person.

Being *receptive* means you hear and listen to another's
perspective. You are *aware* that you may not have all the answers
yourself. When you are receptive, you are looking for the information you need to accomplish more in your life and become the
person you are meant to be. You are also looking for what you
need, where you might find it, and who could be supplying that
you need.

Willingness is *openness* to attempt something new or adopt
another's perspective. It's also being open to new ideas for the
sake of accomplishing what you want to achieve. Not every idea
is the right choice for you. The important aspect is your willingness to put forth the effort to consider it. The state of being
willing is easy for others to see in you and difficult to recognize
in yourself.

Maybe you are like me. You know you are meant for more
and still can't quite figure out how to attain it. If you tend to keep

moving forward, try new things, and believe in your heart that you are meant for greatness, get ready to be energized.

Without a doubt, you are more than enough. You can be everything you want to be. You can do anything you want to do. This world offers you the opportunity to achieve anything you want. It takes a village of people to reach your fullest potential. To provide that support, we started a nonprofit that focuses on helping people get what they want in life by providing the tools and connections they need to get there. We want to support you on your journey as you follow your passion and build your life of abundance.

GRASP is Powered by Women. We want to encourage *you to pursue your passions and purpose. We exist to help you thrive and to be the best version of yourself that you can be. The more we can encourage and support you, the greater things you can do. It's within your GRASP.*

The core value of abundance and its mindset come from the core of the phrase we use for our nonprofit: **Be More. Do More. Achieve More.**

Our deepest desire is for you to live your life of more, your life of abundance. If you are like us, you will never give up on your quest to live your life to the fullest. This book will help you get started from where you are currently. It will give you many of the skills and the mindset you need along your journey.

Life does not happen in isolation. I used to think that I could change my whole world by reading the right book or learning the right skills. Now I understand why I couldn't transform myself until after learning how to open up and let people care for and help me. Thankfully, my life is now full of deep, lasting friendships. It took learning how to share myself and let others into my life to experience true abundance. I desire that you experience this as well. I want you to Be More, Do More, and Achieve More.

Through my desire to help people live their lives of abundance, I have had the opportunity to hear people reveal dreams that they have carried inside their hearts for years. I have been fortunate to walk alongside them to develop and promote those dreams. Working toward your goals benefits everyone involved and provides space for everyone to thrive. We want to value you. We want to encourage you to follow the dreams and passions in your heart. We are here for you.

If you want to learn more and connect with a group of people who are just like you, please check out our Facebook page:

https://www.facebook.com/GiveforStrength
or visit our website at www.grasp.gives
or check us out on Instagram @grasp.gives

You can always reach us by email at grasp.gives@gmail.com. We look forward to connecting with you.

Section I

Mindset and Preparation

1

Live Your Life in the Wilderness

If any of you lacks wisdom,
let him ask God who gives generously to all without reproach,
and it will be given to him.
(James 1:5 ESV)

BRENÈ BROWN USES the concept of "braving the wilderness" in her book by that name. Brown says braving the wilderness means true belonging. It is the spiritual practice of believing in and belonging to yourself so deeply that you can share your most authentic self with the world and find sacredness in both being part of something and standing alone in the wilderness. **True belonging doesn't require you to *change* who you are; it requires you to *be* who you are.**

The wilderness can be a beautiful place generally untouched by humans and "human progress." The ecosystem in the wilderness, as chaotic as it might be and without human help, works because each element has a different role or purpose. The fox does not play the part of the flowers, and the pine tree does not play the role of the rabbits. How I wish we could know what roles we play in the world and be proud and strong in our convictions of what our roles are. We often try to be what everyone else wants us to be, but it ends up harming our ecosystem, our life, our marriages, and our jobs. Just like gaps in a plant and animal ecosystem create imbalances, so does a lack of purpose in our own lives.

I deeply long for you to have true belonging in your life, to know who you are, and to be brave and confident enough to stand up and live your authentic life. An authentic life leads to an abundant life. I believe in you. It will be hard. It may get uncomfortable. You will want to give up and go back to your old ways. Know that I believe in you. Give yourself a little pep talk, and be kind and gracious to yourself. We all make mistakes. We all get down and discouraged with ourselves at times. Unfortunately, we all do things that we wish we hadn't. We all fail at times in what we have tried to do. What sets you apart from the masses is your ability to get back up and keep moving forward.

For some of us, maybe we have put forth a great deal of effort to accomplish something incredibly important to us, but it failed. That is difficult, and it might be hard to get back up and attempt something again. That "mistake" that you made, or that thing that didn't quite work out the way you intended, may not have been a mistake at all. What if you needed to learn to get to the next place you are going? Things that feel like failures to us sometimes aren't failures at all. It could have taught you something. It could have taught you multiple lessons for the challenges along the way. You can do it—keep moving, get up, and get back in the game. You've got this.

Let me share a personal story that may give you the strength to keep going and push you toward your abundant life.

I worked with a company as an independent contractor for over seven years and had minimal success, even after going full-time with the company. Everyone I knew believed in me, and everyone else thought that I could be extremely successful in areas such as income, the people I could help, and the size of the business I could build.

My husband was especially supportive in my quest to achieve recognition and make a lot of money. I felt that he desired that I meet his and everyone else's expectations of success. I also believed that I could do what it took to meet everyone else's expectations, but I did not do it. Whenever I had a small measure of success, I would subconsciously sabotage my results, and my progress would tank. This action would shift my internal dialogue into a negative spiral, and I spent countless hours searching for the underlying reasons why I had so many "issues."

Eventually, I began to think that I was doing the wrong thing and started to pinball all over the place with ideas of other opportunities I could or should do that would be a better fit. Of course, my husband, who had previously been so supportive, began to tease me and to doubt my ability to accomplish what I said I would do. My self-talk got even worse at this point. I was guilt-ridden and depressed most of the time, and I felt like a loser. Luckily, I did not give up.

It's important to me that I share with you what I have learned. After investing years into reading books, attending seminars, listening to speakers, undergoing therapy, practicing self-reflection, participating in group processes, and enrolling in graduate school for coaching and understanding how humans change and grow, I finally feel confident enough to share what I have learned with you. The steps to finding your true passion were created through my struggles. I know they work because it took me years to change how I was attempting to move against the flow of my own life. My greatest hope is that you will experience the same transformation that I have experienced in my life.

While I was attempting to follow someone else's direction and goals for my life, my subconscious mind saw a different life for myself deep down. I was subconsciously sabotaging myself to put myself back into my rightful place in the world. Many people experience struggles and deep pain from their past and don't even recognize it. Your self-sabotaging ways may be an effort to protect you from pain, and you don't even notice that there is something in your past directing your actions.

You may not be at a place in your life where this is the case or where awareness of that information is useful. It depends much on your family of origin and how you responded to pains in your life. If you feel that something deeper is blocking your progress and you are open to exploring further, we will cover some of the challenges and awareness in a later chapter.

As it turned out, I had been frustrated, negative, and upset with myself because I was not meeting someone else's definition of success. On top of that, I was guilt-ridden and depressed most of the time because "I was such a loser."

After pulling "**my life**" out of my subconscious mind, I no longer had any guilt or negative feelings toward the choices that I was making. I knew everything I had done so far in my life was not a waste. It set up the intellectual framework for what would come next and for accomplishing what I am supposed to do in this world. Finding my purpose was part of the journey, struggles, and pain.

I realized peace in every aspect of my life—peace with my husband, with my child, in my business, with my current financial situation, and most importantly, in my spiritual life.

My life was supposed to include the current company where I worked. It was a stepping stone to everything else I was destined to become. I had just been focusing on the wrong things. As soon as I had peace in my life and the correct focus, my business plans grew in the right direction. I began to work one step at a time toward my purpose and passions in my life. What a miracle! Life is great and abundant.

It doesn't matter who you are right now.

What matters is who you become on the journey.

Living your life of abundance is not about money or getting rich quickly. Money is a tool that you can use to make your life easier. The definition of abundance is a large quantity of something, the state or condition of having a copious quantity of something, or plentifulness of the good things in life. Living your life of abundance is living with a plentiful amount of good things and having the fullness of all good things overflowing.

Many people equate abundance only to money or wealth. Abundance relates to every area of your life. You can have an abundance of joy, influence, opportunity, blessing, love, grace, friendship, kindness, and anything else that you desire. By living in abundance, you will have the full, rich life that you deserve. You will be living a life full of blessings and favor, which is what God desires for you.

My desire for you is to live your life filled with an abundance of love, joy, peace, happiness, health, passion, focus, purpose, excellence, blessings, friendship, and freedom. Having abundance encapsulates every area of your life. You deserve to live **your** life of abundance. It's what God intends for you, and I pray you will receive it by reading this book.

Know Your Purpose

Being your authentic self means knowing your purpose, which allows you to focus more on others and less on yourself. Your purpose comes from within you rather than a motivation for external or superficial gratification. Your purpose is your "why" for your life, and it is the reason you get up in the morning. In *The Power of Significance*, John Maxwell wrote, "God gives purpose. Purpose gives meaning. Meaning gives hope and significance."

Knowing and understanding your purpose gives you a reason to keep moving forward. You will feel joy in any circumstance because you will focus on internal motivation. With purpose, your life has meaning despite the setbacks of the moment. There is less doubt or fleeting confidence in what you are doing when things go poorly, and you become joy-filled and significant in all circumstances.

When you don't know or understand your "why," you have to spend a lot of time looking for it and figuring it out. It is something that most of us have had to go through, and it is part of your journey and a normal part of life. The process takes time and effort, which can be discouraging at times. It can change the trajectory of your life when you know your "why." It will be worth the effort for you and everyone you interact with now and in the future to figure it out.

Throughout this process, you will be focused on yourself while attempting to find your purpose. When you are young, you focus on figuring out what you want in life and who you are. It is a blessing to have someone in your life who can reflect on what you are doing well and steer you in the right direction. Often, the need for external validation is present, which is beneficial, and it helps you know what you are good at doing and not good at doing.

When you get an idea of your purpose, your focus begins to shift outward to others rather than yourself. The sooner you know what your why is, the sooner you can take your primary focus away from yourself and place your emphasis on others, and that is where your purpose turns into significance. Your significance is the place that motivates you to keep moving forward.

It makes me think of a new salesperson. It is a tough place to be, a young person needing money to survive, and he often learns to view sales as a commission rather than an opportunity to help people. The trap of earning a commission has ended many new sales jobs rather quickly, and it is difficult to keep up the energy for it. It is especially true when the salesperson's heart isn't into "earning a commission." A salesperson can easily shift the purpose of selling from "self-focus," which is getting a commission, to "others" focus. When a sale brings the opportunity to help people with their needs and to solve someone *else's problem*, everyone wins.

> ### <u>Focus Change Experiment</u>
>
> **Choose to be a blessing to someone this week and every week, whether you think they need it or not.**
>
> - Bring someone coffee or breakfast
> - Invite someone to lunch
> - Put a flower on the desk of someone you work with
> - Offer to pick up someone's kids or take them home
>
> Make a difference wherever you are.
> Bloom where you are planted.

Several years ago, I met an incredibly nice man who did online reporting for *The Business Journal* in our town. He asked me to do an interview. I focused my time on the questions he supplied because *I wanted it to be a successful interview.* I did not want to look like a fool when he tried to edit the interview footage and realize that I did not leave him with enough good clips to make it worthwhile and waste his time by making the editing job painful. It seems that I had an "other's" focus, but really, it was a "self-focus."

After the interview, things became clearer to me as we talked on the way to his car. The comment he repeated finally made sense. "I hope this helps you out," he said. What I realized as he drove away was the work he does is to highlight people who can benefit from the interview and their organization. What an amazing turn of events. I was humbled to have experienced such an opportunity for him to pour kindness into me. As he turned the corner, leaving my house, what went through my mind was how much joy he must experience in every aspect of his job. What a joyful experience to look for people to help. Do you think he is excited about and has anticipation for who he will get to interview next? It must be fun to put together the right clips to place another person into the spotlight. It must be simple to have joy when you focus on another person and help make his job and life better, easier, or more successful.

Getting Started

Finding your purpose will take some time and introspection. You can download a journal and free resources at www.margospilde.com/resources. Your first step is to get a fresh notebook or journal ready. Your life of abundance starts here; it's where your future begins to take shape. Your most important tool will be your journal. You may want to use a computer or portable electronic device if that is what you are most comfortable using. However, you will want to access it quickly and frequently, so find the system that works best for you that is always quick and easy to access.

The exercises in this book are very simple and straightforward. The most important ingredient to your success will be how truthful and thoughtful you are with your answers. You will see results when you go through these exercises with sincere intent and an honest approach. This book will alter your current reality, and it can lead you to the right road to living your life of abundance.

In writing this book, I intended to create a comprehensive, easy-to-understand, and useful tool that will inspire you to find your true passion in life. The tools discussed here will lead and encourage you to find your true passion as you walk through the steps to discovery. There is a way to move forward even if you have no money, are completely in debt, and have failed at everything else. You can experience a life of abundance in all areas of your life—spiritual, emotional, relational, intellectual (career), financial, and physical. Throughout the steps of discovery, you will gain additional clarity and receive practical, useful steps. It's time to stop wishing and start living your desired life of abundance.

You have probably never consciously thought about the questions I am about to ask you, so as your subconscious mind gets a hold of them, you will repeatedly have thoughts popping into your head. Make sure you immediately write down any thoughts that come up or ideas you have when you think of them. These thoughts will likely be an important part of your future.

Write down every thought that comes to mind. It does not matter how trivial. You may think that one of your strengths or likes sounds silly. Maybe you believe something you dislike is not pertinent. You will be surprised how ridiculous items that come up may be key to understanding your passion and future. They may not be silly at all after considering them alongside all of your thoughts and ideas.

An example of something that I could have left off my list is that I love to organize. I could spend hours organizing a room or my whole house, or someone else's house, for that matter. To most people, this is a complete waste of time. This strange hobby is not likely to be a windfall career choice, but after I wrote it down in my strength category, I let my subconscious mind work on it. After a while, I began to see how important this trait was to find my true passions in life. Anything I chose to do in my future had to involve organizing, or at the very least, my propensity to spend time organizing could not be hindered.

I know an amazing person who has made a successful business and career out of organizing. She may have thought, as I did, that it wasn't a useful skill. Maybe people gave her a hard time when she decided to turn organizing into a business. However, this woman was brave and bold enough to follow her passion despite anyone else's thoughts or opinions. Bravery is an admirable character trait. I would guess that she often didn't feel brave. There were probably times that she thought she had made a mistake in starting her business. Yet she kept moving forward. Don't let doubts and discouragement create a roadblock for you. Instead, weave around the cones like a NASCAR driver dodging debris on the track.

All the things you love or dislike doing will be part of your decision to pursue or not pursue certain avenues in your life. I realized that anything I chose to do should involve organizing, and if it didn't, I might not enjoy it enough for it to become a passion.

Excuses and Lies

You may feel that because you have not seen the results you wanted so far in your life, there is something wrong with you. Sometimes I hear people talk about their fear of success or say why success, wealth, or a better life just isn't for them. That is a classic excuse for permitting yourself to give up.

It is easy to blame or label something when you haven't done what you should have done. That's the typical middle-class way of thinking in America. It is someone else's fault that you didn't get what you wanted. What if you didn't get what you wanted based on the outcome of your choices? You didn't get the promotion because you did not perform at your highest level on the last project. The choices you made were to take a long lunch once or twice per week and scroll through social media when nobody was around to see what you were doing.

You are lying to yourself when you say you didn't get the promotion because your boss doesn't like you; she's been out to get you for years, and this was her chance. The lies you tell yourself are destructive, and they keep you stuck. They allow you to place the results of your life in someone else's power. But you must start believing that you have control and authority over your own life. When you blame someone else or use the excuse that it won't be that great anyway, it permits you to put forth little effort.

I want you to know that it's worth it. Traveling and seeing the world is worth it. Saying yes when your kids ask for something they want is worth it. Having the freedom to buy pre-cut vegetables or sliced cheese is worth it. Not using a calculator in the grocery store or purchasing expensive jeans that fit just right is worth it. Stop making excuses and do something about it. A little progress each day adds up to big results. You can have whatever you want in life. It is better than you ever imagined it might be, and you can turn things around quickly.

You may have "not done it" so many times in your life or let your family down so often that they have lost faith in you. The biggest problem is that you have lost faith in yourself. We often learn as young children that it is acceptable not to follow through on our intentions. Change that pattern right now. Start by setting small goals for yourself that you know you can accomplish. You will slowly begin a habit of following through on what you tell yourself you are going to do.

If you have made a habit of letting yourself down, you know you will not follow through on commitments to yourself. Change that habit right now, and follow through, or there is no point in deciding to do anything new. Nothing will change until you learn not to let yourself get away with it. Choose to have the highest integrity with yourself first.

Encouragement

Your current reality is only that—your current reality. It does not mean this is your destiny forever. Now is your chance to make your life different. Do not skip a word of this book. Get a journal and do the exercises. I promise your life is going to be changed forever. You can't follow this process and not change for the better.

Journaling is an excellent enhancement to your current reality. It helps you document what you told yourself you would do and record how far you have come. A journal keeps a logbook of where you were and where you are going. Continue following these steps and writing down your intentions, dreams, and desires. You will not be able to forget what you told yourself when you write it down in your journal.

Success Tips:

- Every three to five years, update or redo the steps in Chapter 4; start with the end in mind.
- Journal your goals and dreams regularly. Your thoughts, dreams, and visions will get bigger as you grow personally. Eventually, this will become a habit, not a process.
- Track your success in your journal, too!
- Write down ideas that come to your mind. You will be surprised at what comes out of your ideas, reflections, and random thoughts.
- Your subconscious mind is a powerful tool. It will find answers to the questions you ask. Do good things in the world and for you and your family.

Enjoy your journey.

2

Live Your Life with Passion

Delight yourself in the LORD
and he will give you the desires of your heart.
(Psalm 37:4, ESV)

THE BIGGEST CHALLENGE for most people is knowing what they want. It's virtually impossible to get somewhere if you don't know where you are going. If you don't know, invest your time figuring out where your passions lie. What you do next is extremely important. Decide what is important to you. Then write it down because you are likely to forget. Write down action steps to achieve what you want, and most importantly, take some action. Do something, do anything—just get started.

What Is Your Motivation?

Deep down, you want your life to matter. You want to do something in the world that gets noticed and shows that you are a success. To get there, you need lots of passion for where you are going. Motivation is the passion or the "gas" in the engine that drives you toward living a life of abundance. The passion is what gets you up in the morning, and it's what carries you through the difficult days. Without passion and purpose, you will find it difficult to get anywhere significant.

Your motivation can be one of the biggest determining factors in your joy in life. Success can result from doing what you love and finding your purpose. You can feel successful in your life independent of whether or not others judge you to be a success. When you live your life in the wilderness, believing in and belonging to yourself so deeply that you can share your most authentic self with the world, you can live in joy, and it won't matter what others believe about you.

Success can also come to those who have somewhat selfish motives. An example of this is a person who performs to be seen as significant or is motivated to please people. Highly influential people can often appear extremely successful. Do you think they are experiencing joy? Are they stressed and unhappy because of the burden of attempting to live up to the expectations of others? Someone else's life may look perfect from the outside. You often don't know what is happening underneath the surface or behind closed doors.

It is important to mention that highly influential people who appear successful, or those who claim to be people-pleasers, can also be filled with joy. What is at the core of their motivation to act is not readily apparent to others. It is a very personal topic to look at within yourself. Decide what motivates you and be aware if you receive questionable results that cause less joy in your life.

After further studying your motivation, it can appear to be one thing on the surface but turn out to be something else. We once had an employee who informed me that her purpose was to please others. This was extremely important to her, and it was what motivated her in her work every day. I believed what she told me. Eventually, the working relationship became uncomfortable when I made a request for her to stop doing a specific task. It got especially unpleasant when my preferences did not align with what she wanted to do. The relationship ended with her walking out and dumping a year's worth of grievances on me that she had never expressed previously. As it turned out, her need to please people was likely rooted in her need for validation and approval.

On the outside, what appeared to be the socially acceptable personality trait of people-pleasing may have had a more personal motivation. She was not aware of her own needs and motivations and was not experiencing joy in her life. Things were uncomfortable for me. I had no idea why I was experiencing the angst and did not understand what was going on with her. If she had understood and recognized her motivation, which is called "awareness," she may have experienced greater joy and happiness in her job without causing a loss in the relationship.

Strategies to begin pinpointing your underlying motivations:

1. Verbalize your need to someone else.
2. Discuss things that bother you at home and work.
3. Recognize what is eliminating your joy.
4. Make efforts to give yourself the validation and approval you need.
5. Be responsible for meeting your needs.
6. Care for and nurture yourself when you are hurting.
7. Take action when a relationship needs to be restored.
8. Apologize when it's appropriate for your part in the situation.

It is sad to watch people destroy relationships because of their pain. It is even harder to sit back and watch people create hurt in themselves. You will eliminate much pain for yourself and suffering by those around you by being aware of your needs, asking safe people for what you need, and not believing you are responsible for meeting unexpressed needs of others.

> ### <u>Action Question</u>
>
> ### What motivates you to be your most productive, most joyful self?
>
> - When you become aware of what energizes you the most, you will recognize more quickly what you should keep doing
> - Notice what stops you from being your most effective and positive self to quickly identify and change what hinders you most

I need to have order in my surroundings to feel productive and joyful. I hate clutter. My brain seems to run on overdrive when I'm in a cluttered space. I do not feel calm or peaceful, and it is difficult to focus. I have a strong desire to clean the kitchen at night, and I do not want to wake up to clutter. I cook while cleaning, and I would prefer to clean before I sit down to eat. I may have a problem.

With three kids, pets, and a spouse leaving stuff around the house, I was experiencing a major lack of joy. At first, there seemed to be only two options to solve my challenge. Option one involved spending much of my time picking up things that other people had left around the house and not accomplishing my tasks. Option two included a bunch of yelling at everyone and chasing the dog around the house while she took out the toys I had already picked up.

Once I identified how much of a motivator an uncluttered environment was for me, I embraced and added option three. It required a large time investment, and the results were excellent. We decluttered the entire house and every storage area. We sold stuff and donated stuff. Every giant bag that went out to the trash was euphoric for me. I am more creative, more focused, and more available for my family, and I love being in this space now. {I know some great organizers if you need any help in this area.}

Ask for What You Want

Long ago, *The Secret* was a popular informational video that featured famous authors and motivational speakers who shared "the secret." Maybe you read or heard about it. Step one in *The Secret* is about asking for what you want. **Ask** for what you desire in your life, and you may very well get it. If you don't ask, you will likely not get what you want.

Mark Batterson, in his book *Draw the Circle*, uses a different term. Spell it out, he says. It is the same way Jesus asked the question of two blind men: "What do you want me to do for you?" in Matthew 20:32. It is a crucial question. Jesus already knew these men were searching for Him to be healed of their blindness, yet He made them verbalize specifically what they wanted Him to do.

It isn't easy to ask for what you need or want from your spouse, kids, boss, friends, coworkers—the list goes on and on. I have been married for over twenty-five years. We have three kids, pets, jobs, and responsibilities. It is pure chaos much of the time. At one point in the chaos, I told my kids and spouse what I wanted for gifts. Eventually, I started buying my own gifts because that was easier than my husband trying to find them later. I would say, "Here is my gift for the next occasion." Sometimes the kids would wrap them up, which would make it a surprise for everyone.

Initially, my husband appeared irritated, and he would buy gifts in addition to what I had bought. That, unfortunately, did not allow me, a very frugal person, much opportunity to choose to be pleasant at gift opening time.

As things progressed, my husband got more on board with my gift buying, and our communication improved around gifts. What happened next? My husband got fewer and very boring gifts because we didn't know what he wanted. The rest of us had a joyous time getting exactly what we asked for. Unfortunately, since my husband did not ask for anything, he ended up not getting what he wanted.

My daughter attempted to make sure that we got her dad something that he would love, but it still did not match the enthusiasm from those who *loved* what they had received after expressing their desires. One Christmas, he decided to tell us what he REALLY wanted! He had so much excitement about the gift he had chosen. We heard about, talked about, and got to experience his binder machine more than we could have ever imagined. The best part was that he truly loved what he had gotten as a gift. Seriously, there was zero chance that anyone would have come up with the idea of buying him a binding machine for Christmas like the ones they use at the FedEx or UPS stores. It still makes him happy to bind anything that might need to be bound.

What if someone asked you, "What do you want me to do for you?" Would you know how to answer, or would you stammer while trying to figure out exactly what it is that you want? When people would ask me what they could do for me, my typical response had been to say, "Nothing." So I got what I asked for— nothing. I probably missed out on many opportunities from people who wanted to help me or bless me. Do you have an idea of what you want? Can you specifically say what you want in your life? Start deciding what you want and speaking your needs to others. Start right away, because it will take a lot of practice.

If you don't know what you want, you can't ask for it. That was my biggest challenge. I did not know what I wanted. That is likely one of the biggest reasons many people go from one self-help program to another. I have read or attempted to read hundreds of self-help books. Almost all of them were great with lots of useful information, but my life still did not change.

> ### Call to Action
>
> **Decide what you want or need from others
> and speak your need to someone you can trust
> to respond affirmingly and with kindness.**
>
> - Make a decision about what you need
> - Ask someone to meet your need
> - Do it again, because you will need a lot of
>   practice to become good at it

What you will read here is designed to walk you through the steps of discovering what you want in life. Once you have figured out what you want, the rest of the book supports achieving what you want and aids you in bringing about and maintaining *your* **life of abundance.** If you do these exercises, you will be on a path to finding peace, happiness, joy, and love in all areas of your life. My hope is for you to stop wishing, wondering, and wandering through life with less than you deserve. Let's get started.

Decide What You Want

What is it that you want to accomplish in your life? Most people merely exist because they don't know what they want or where they are going. The two most important questions you will answer for yourself are:

- What do I want?
- Why do I want it?

Let's say you have the week off. You load up the kids and all the stuff in the car that you will need.

As you start to drive away, the kids are excited and ask, "Where are we going?"

Your response is, "I don't know. We will find out when we get there."

You drive for a while and exit off the road. Nothing is interesting at that location, so you get back on the highway. You try a few more exits and drive a few different routes. After a while, you find a place to have lunch and see that the family is reluctant to return to the car. Hours after coaxing the kids back into the car, you come across a small carnival and spend a couple of hours there before looking for a hotel for the night. Every day you get up to do the same thing—drive somewhere hoping to find something to do.

Throughout the week, you stayed in some nice and some not-so-nice hotels. You had some good meals and some just OK meals. You even found a few fun things to do along the way, but what did you do?

Everybody asks, "Where did you go on your vacation?" when you get back to work.

What is your response? "Nowhere, I guess."

"What did you do?"

"Nothing, really."

"Did you have fun?"

"Yeah, I guess we did."

You didn't go anywhere or do anything in particular, and you took up an entire week to do it. Did you have a positive experience? You enjoyed your family, but what came from it? A mediocre vacation that no one will remember unless someone asks, "Remember that time we went nowhere for vacation?"

Is that how you want your life to be—a series of somewhat enjoyable experiences amidst the frustration of getting back into the car and going to work? If the answer is no, then isn't it time you did something about it?

Five Steps to Discover Your Desires

Make sure you have your journal available. Before answering, write each question down or use the pre-printed journal on our website. You can access a digital copy at http://margospilde.com/resources for the journal and additional resources. If you are using a blank journal, write each step on a separate page or skip a page, so you have plenty of room to write and continue to record thoughts that pop into your head.

1. What are my strengths?

- What are you good at doing? Think beyond skills at your job.
- What are you naturally good at doing? Sometimes this can be tough; those things come so easily and can be hard to notice.
- Ask your friends and family what they think you are especially good at doing. Often, the people close to us notice gifts that we don't recognize in ourselves.
- What are your hobbies?
- What do you like doing on your long weekends?
- What are some of your general strengths that seem unrelated to any job you may have done?

This point is where I contemplated my strength of organizing. Although I love doing it, it seemed to be a wasted talent. However, when I got into this project, I realized how important the strength of organizing is to anything I decide to do.

2. What do I love to do?

- What is it that you are doing when time flies by for hours?

- What are you doing when you stay awake all night or wake up early to do?

Keep going on questions one and two; these could be long lists. Be honest with yourself. See how good it feels to think about the things that you love? These are the things that make your blood surge through your veins. Many items will be on both lists; that's OK. You are writing out the truth of who you are. If any business or potential work ideas pop into your head, write them in the margin somewhere, so you don't forget. Keep feeling the authentic person, _the person that you are_, come alive on paper.

3. What do I truly hate doing?

- What are your least favorite tasks at work?
- What tasks have you decided to let your spouse manage in the family (or wish your spouse would take over for you)?
- Are there particular jobs around the house or special projects that you should not oversee?
- What projects do you do poorly, feel are always mediocre, or simply can never do well?

When a task is something you dislike, you may not do it anyway. That is procrastination, or you will do it grudgingly because you feel forced. It's OK to not like something; write those things down too, so you can eliminate as many hated items as possible.

You know what I hate doing? Painting. Yes, the walls look great with a new coat of paint. Yes, painters are expensive. Nope, I am not going to bother doing it, no matter what. You cannot convince me that it will be easy or quick. No way! I know that I hate painting, and I am really bad at it. As a real estate investor, it might be easy to get sucked into the money-saving plan of not hiring a painter, except I hate painting. That will always go into the budget. Put those things you hate to do on your list and make your life much less stressful.

One of my kids asked me the other day, "Remember that thing I told you I hated? I told you I hated it my whole life, and look at what we wrote down when I was in preschool. I hated it then, too." I stood corrected as a mom. Yes, you have hated that your entire life. Children know what they like and what they hate. I have given up attempting to make them try it again or see if they have changed their minds. Nope, nada, ain't gonna happen. That is not their bag, and nothing I say will make any difference. What is the one thing you will gladly pay any amount of money to keep yourself from having to do? Isn't it time, as adults, that we stand up against what we hate to do? Sometimes we need to do things that we don't love or don't prefer doing. That is entirely different from what you strongly dislike. Even on a good day, it will get done poorly if you feel there is no choice. Vacuuming or dusting—I wouldn't say I like doing those things, but that's life.

Call to Action

It's OK to not like something and want to avoid it!

- Write down these things so you recognize them
- Immediately eliminate the things you dislike and hate doing

---

4. What do I never seem to get around to doing?

- What things do I procrastinate on the most?
- Which items never seem to get crossed off the list?
- What do people constantly have to ask you to finish?

Do you want to write a book, start an internet company, or small businesses? Is there a different career or field you want to be in? The possibilities are endless. If you don't have many ideas initially, your mind will start to work on this subject, and you will be surprised what grand ideas your brain thinks up.

Call to Action

What have you put off doing?

- Think about your family, job, children, and goals, and write down things you haven't gotten to yet
- Do you have a business idea that you haven't pursued?
- Is there a project you have procrastinated working on?
- What have you started and never finished?

Procrastination is a bad habit stemming from fear and doubt. It can reflect deeper hurts and wounds that dictate your choices. It may also be a thought process that your brain created to protect yourself from old pain, but it no longer serves you well. Continued procrastination is often a clue about things you don't enjoy doing.

5. **What discrepancies do I see with my current career path?**

- What do I dislike most about my current career?
- What are the things I love most about my career?
- What have I always wanted to do or be?
- Will my current career allow me to grow professionally and provide intellectual development?

Take note of your observations in this area. Are there key duties in your job that fall into your list of despised activities? Realize this may be one of the main reasons you are not as successful as you would like to be. Instead of beating yourself up about your lack of success, now you can feel great about having this awareness, and you have the power to take steps to change it. You are in control of all the decisions and choices you have taken so far in your life. Be thankful for the opportunities you have experienced so far and what you have learned about life and yourself.

We all do things we don't want or like doing; that is just part of life. However, if you are attempting to build your life and success around activities that you try to avoid doing, you can now see that your success will be much slower at the very least and maybe non-existent.

While working at my first job out of college, we were mandated to read *Soar with your Strengths* by Donald O. Clifton and Paula Nelson. The ideas in the book made so much sense to me. If you spend your time getting better at what you like doing and are naturally good at doing, you can become great at it. However, if you invest hours and hours working on getting better at things you don't enjoy and aren't good at doing, you will likely only become mediocre at best, and it will have taken much of your time, energy, and effort to get there.

Although the book was supposed to make me better at my current career, it started my path to figure out what I was supposed to be doing later in life. I closed the book and thought, "Why am I working here?" I spent sixty hours or more per week managing teenagers at Target and realized that this was not what I wanted to be doing in ten, fifteen, or twenty years.

After reading that book, it still took me more than ten years to figure out what I wanted to be when I grew up. I want you to soar, and I hope it happens much sooner for you. Keep in mind that it will happen for you only when you use your strengths and passions. Your excitement and enthusiasm are the biggest factors in your ability to succeed. **Enthusiasm is authentic. Enthusiasm is transferable.** You want to feel the way you do when you show up excited. Love life, love what you do, and have great joy in everything.

Well-intended people will tell you to just get it done. Do whatever it takes to get it done where you are currently, and eventually you will become good at it. That is true to some extent, and it becomes a problem only when you are completely on the wrong track. Yes, you can become good at anything, and as your success grows, you will probably need and want to do some of the things currently on your list of undesirables. However, start by building upon your strengths.

As you grow and experience small successes, you will find it easier to learn new skills, and at times, those things you hate or procrastinate about now may become things you are good at and enjoy doing. Growth is a healthy way to live. Learn to embrace growth and transformation as it happens.

3

Live Your Life with Clarity

If you know these things,
blessed are you if you do them.
(John 13:17, NKJV)

WHAT IS YOUR current reality? Did you learn to look at the world negatively from your family of origin? It is challenging to unlearn those habits that were formed early.

- What is it that you don't like about your life currently?
- What is it that you don't want?

Odds are you will be able to list dozens of items that you do not want or like about your life with very little effort. We are often more aware of what we don't want and have little understanding or emotion to figure out what we do want. Therefore, what you will be doing next is harnessing greater emotion and passion toward discovering what you want.

Six Steps to a Clear Vision

Step One: What do you not like about your life currently?

Start a list—I'm serious. Write down everything you no longer want in your life. Draw a line down the middle of your paper for two vertical columns. In step one, you will use the column on the

29

left side. Remember to leave room on the right-side column for the next step.

Below this heading, you will list the things you don't like about your life. At the top, write down "I do not want" and underline it twice. If you need more room to write, draw a second column on the next page. You will use the columns to compare and contrast, so don't skip drawing the line down the middle.

Idea Prompts: "I do not want."

- What do you not like about your life currently?
- What things do you want to change?
- Is there something that you don't like about your job or career?
- If you could eliminate items from your life, what would they be?
- What are you afraid might happen to you?
- What do you hate doing?

Write down absolutely everything you do not wish to have in your life.

After you have exhausted all of your thoughts on that subject, you may want to **continue your list with "I hate."** It could stir up emotions about more things you do not want in your life.

The following was an actual example from my life when I went through this process of self-reflection. My statements will give you an idea of the process, how it works, and how to channel your thoughts.

Example:

- I do not want to be mandated to be anywhere at any time.
- I do not want to be told what I can or can't do.
- I do not want to ask anyone if I can leave town or not.

- I do not want to make decisions based on whether I can afford it or not.
- I do not want my children to think their mom doesn't do anything.
- I do not want my children raised by someone else.
- I do not want to leave the house at the crack of dawn.
- I do not want to drive in rush-hour traffic regularly.
- I do not want to be at the end of my life knowing that I did nothing for humanity and made no difference in the world.
- I do not want to be impatient with my children.
- I do not want to snap at my children or be short with them.
- I do not want to worry about money, ever.

Put all of your efforts into step number one. Don't skip out or think you will write down a few things and do more later. I read this list years after I had originally written it, and I felt a fire of excitement and passion rise inside of me. Every statement on that list was still true for me ten to fifteen years later. My life was different, and many of those items had come true, yet I had grown complacent because life was good to me, and I rarely had to deal with those negatives.

Write them down, and your subconscious may direct and push you to achieve a life where you avoid getting the items you do not want. I was very passionate about not driving to work in morning traffic. It also seemed that anything I pushed myself to attend in the morning did not fulfill me or add to my enjoyment of life. There are not many opportunities that are worth eliminating my peaceful morning routine or enduring morning traffic. Therefore, I have decided not to go anywhere in the early morning, and I avoid driving in rush-hour traffic.

Life is amazing. Our brains are amazing. You can design your life to be exactly how you want it. You can have anything and everything you want in life when you decide what that is.

Step Two: What is the opposite of each item listed on the left side of your page?

Write down the exact opposite of what you do not want on the opposite side of the paper.

Write a contrasting statement of what you do not want on the right side of your columns. Write it in the positive and present tense. This step needs no emotions or thinking. You will simply write an opposing statement for each item on the list of things you don't want and hate doing.

The new list will give you a good idea of what you want in your life. Once you know these things, you will begin attaching emotions to them in later steps.

Start your list with "I" or "My." You can write more than one positive statement for each negative as I have done below. Typically, a thing you hate will elicit more than one negative emotion or activity you don't like, so let the positives flow through you.

Example:

- I make a choice to go anywhere I want in the world.
- I choose when I want to go places.
- I make my own choices 100 percent of the time.
- I go anywhere in the world I want, anytime I want.
- I buy anything I want.
- I do everything I want to do.
- My lucrative career improves the lives of everyone with whom I do business.
- I am the biggest influence in my children's lives.
- I work when and where I want to work.
- My decisions impact the world every day.
- I make the world a better place to live.
- I am patient and understanding with my children.
- I am financially free.

- I have enough passive income to pay for my desired lifestyle.

It is important to write your statements in a way that indicates the goal has been achieved. For example, do not write "I will" do something. It sets you up for a letdown if you have created the habit of not following through on commitments to yourself and you don't accomplish what you said you will do. At first, you may not believe what you have written. If it feels like a lie, and your brain contradicts each statement. You will want to word it in a manner that does not feel like a lie. Here is an example from my life and how I turned the wording around to make it more believable and powerful.

Example: *I am buying $2.5 million in real estate **this year.***

What if it's October? If I hadn't bought anything that year, the time frame felt hopeless. The wording *this year* was problematic for me in multiple ways. If the internal drive to achieve my goal is more important than making the right purchase, I will hurt myself more than help. It was an internal struggle between doing the right thing or meeting my goal.

Additionally, I can't control the market. Prices could be over-inflated, the numbers may not work, or the market could become flooded with buying opportunities. How do I manage this confusion, and why am I spending so much time being irritated about it? It felt as if I were always lying to myself because of the calendar year limit, and I wanted to feel motivated to keep moving forward no matter the scenario.

Solution: *I am buying $1.5 million in real estate **in the coming year.***

That gave me a rolling year. My brain believes the goal is possible to achieve any time of the year and in any situation.

Almost any market or buying scenario will work in this rolling twelve-month period. The biggest advantage was eliminating the negative spiral and thoughts that pass when I am not on track or feel hopeless to achieve that goal in the calendar year. With this wording, yesterday is gone, and the focus is on the next twelve-month period. I also lowered the goal because I had attained buying $1.5 million previously. If we purchased another property, the plan would continue to buy a second $1.5 million in the next year.

Step Three: Quantify the items on your list.

Reword the statements from the column on the right side on a new page. Make them specific and eliminate ambiguity. Give each statement you wrote a definite and trackable action. You do not want any vague statements. Each statement must be something that you can get emotionally involved with that motivates you. When money, time, or goals are involved, you want a quantifiable number to track. You want to gauge if or when you have reached your destination. What you are doing now is refining what you **DO** want in your life.

Example:

Things I don't want	Things I do want
"I don't want to be broke"	"I want to have $2,100 to pay our monthly bills and $500 extra to enjoy life"

What exactly do you want?
There must be an absolute number or a trackable result to each statement.

- Do you want to have enough money to pay your bills and have you or your spouse stay home?
- Do you want $500 extra coming in each month to pay down your debt and give yourself peace?
- Do you want to give more to your church or charity? How much do you want to give? Is it $3,000, $7,000, $12,000, or $35,000 per year to your church or other nonprofit groups? Is it $60,000 or more? You get to decide. Make it a believable time frame.
- Do you want to pay for your children's college tuition? Figure out an exact amount for each of your children.
- Do you want to retire your mom or dad from their job in ten months? How much do they need?
- Do you want to be working at the career you love in eight months?
- Do you want to replace or repair your kitchen, bathroom, deck, fence, living room furniture, mattress?
- Do you want to be financially free so you can pursue your dream career and quit your current job in two years?
- Do you want to be a millionaire? Is that one million dollars in cash or one million dollars in assets? How do you quantify and qualify?
- Do you want to have $50,000 or $75,000 or $100,000 or $250,000 or $750,000 in reserves so you can provide security for your family?
- Do you want to have $1,500 a month in passive income?

Since we must have money to live in society, it's important that these examples create a trackable, tangible goal with dollar figures. There are many businesses and objectives that you can use to quantify and motivate you. Narrow your trackable number to the core result you need to achieve your goal and make it a numerical, trackable number.

Personal Example:

One of the goals that I decided to pursue when it seemed we were hopelessly behind for retirement was to reach the milestone of one million dollars in my husband's retirement account. Don't get caught up on the number. Anyone can google maximum 401(k) contribution limits to see the most anyone could contribute during that time frame was $209,500. Essentially, anyone in the United States with a 401(k) plan had the same opportunity to acquire one-half million dollars in a retirement account doing the same thing we did.

We were extremely fortunate to have two retirement accounts, and we chose to fully fund both of them despite the financial markets crashing and the great recession. I have heard a phrase from several people who have achieved the abundance mindset: "Luck is when action meets opportunity." We certainly had both in our favor. The awesome thing is that everyone has the same opportunity to choose abundance, notice opportunities, and decide to take action.

When I set my goal to attain one million dollars, we had small balances in four separate employer accounts. The financial market began increasing substantially, and our balances began to grow. Although I began to see a glimmer of hope, acquiring a substantial retirement balance still felt hopeless. I chose to keep the goal to reach one million dollars despite the immense odds against us. It took an incredibly long time, and I began to doubt that anyone could achieve that goal or retire if it took that long. You get to choose a goal to set for yourself, even if it feels unattainable. Your number might be $100, $500, $1,000, $10,000, $100,000, $1 million, or $10 million. The number is only relevant to your situation, and once you attain it, you get to choose a new number.

We did eventually reach the goal. It was a short-lived window of miraculous proportions because the markets crashed again two weeks later. I could have easily chosen to think small or limit myself when I began to doubt and see how little control I had in the outcome.

Recognize the importance of choosing an exact number, and don't let yourself give up. If you never set the goal, every day will be just another day.

1) Put forth your intention and action toward achieving it.
2) Make your goal measurable and trackable.
3) Make great choices.
4) Follow through with your action plan.
5) Continue to move forward despite disappointments and challenges.

If you continuously move forward with joy and expectation in your heart, you will eventually reach the goals you have set.

Step Four: Clarify and refine the statements on your list.

Once you have quantified your statements, ensure they are written in the present tense and are believable. You will write your statements on a new page to clarify and refine the wording to make it believable and easy to understand. That means the statement will read as if it has already happened for you. Take more time revising and rewriting your words to ensure they are all in the present tense. If you have a lot of similar topics, try to combine them into one statement.

Example *(written as if they have already been achieved):*

- I have $2 million saved in our emergency and retirement accounts.
- I make over $50,000 every year in passive income.
- I am financially free because my passive income is more than my living expenses.
- I positively impact the world every day and improve the lives of everyone with whom I have contact.
- I am the biggest influence in my children's lives.
- I am patient and understanding with my kids. I am a great listener.
- I have no debt except what other people pay for. (I stole this one from Grant Cardone. It's brilliant!!)
- I have the opportunity to choose to travel twice per year to exotic locations.

Step Five: Imagine you achieved each of your statements in your life.

These statements represent your deepest desires. Feel the emotions that achieving each of these in your life creates for you. Set a timer, sit in a comfortable space, close your eyes, and spend at least one minute thinking about or meditating on each statement individually. This step allows you to visualize and emotionalize your wants in your life.

Write down the emotions you are feeling with each one. What thoughts come to your mind? After each one, write down what you are feeling inside and where you experience the emotion, such as your heart, chest, head, entire body, legs, back, etc.

Idea Prompt:

- What does it feel like to have that as your reality?
- See a picture in your mind of how it looks for you.

- Add images and movement.

Everyone visualizes differently, and you may have never done it previously. The following is an example of the process I went through to visualize an item on my list that was rather intangible to start. It may take several practice attempts to feel good about your visualizing skills. Every time you do this, you will catapult your likelihood of success in attaining what you want.

Example: *I have $2 million in our financial freedom accounts.*

First, I see a spreadsheet that tracks investments and progress. Next, I see myself sitting at my computer in my house typing on the spreadsheet. I don't see the words, just the bottom figure—it reads $2,000,321.48. The odd number makes it seem more real, because what is the chance of everything lining up to exactly $2,000,000?

I see myself sitting at the computer, anticipating the number that will come up. I feel the anticipation as I watch this happening in my mind. What do I feel? What do I do when I see the number? I feel the emotions of this happening in my soul. My mind does not know if it is real or pretend.

I see myself running to tell my family and moving excitedly throughout my house. We did it! I see myself picking up the phone to call my husband. I am talking excitedly on the phone and walking quickly around the house. I see myself smiling my biggest smile, and then I sit back in the rocking chair, close my eyes, and reflect upon our accomplishment.

Do this now for one of your desires. How is your attitude different? Are you smiling more? Do you think you may treat your kids differently when you feel this happy? Will you have more patience with your spouse?

Step Six: Take a break.

Let your subconscious mind reflect on the thoughts and the information you have dredged up. It might help to take several opportunities to reflect on different goals on your list. You may also want to repeat some of them and see what else comes up for you. Although you can do all these steps in one sitting, I recommend you stop after this to reflect and allow your mind time to process and develop alternative ideas.

Your mind needs time to process this information. Do something fun with your kids or participate in an activity that you love doing, get your mind on something else, and let your subconscious mind do the work for you. The most important thing you can do right now is **decide you want your life to be different**. Until you decide you will have what you want, this is all just time fillers. If you are reading this to check it off your To-Do list, nothing will ever be different for you.

Have you made the decision?

Great. Now you have figured out the "what," and soon the "how" will follow.

Use the previous statements as your affirmations for goal setting and action planning.

4

Live Your Life in Focus

Ask, and it will be given to you; seek, and you will find;
knock, and it will be opened to you.
For everyone who asks receives, and he who seeks finds,
and to him who knocks, it will be opened.
(Matthew 7:7–8 NKJV)

THE FUTURE YOU see in your mind will be the greatest predictor of what your future will be. Most of us have never taken the time or energy to bring this picture out of our subconscious minds. We haven't given it any clear words or specific images, so we don't know what guides our lives.

Write down your goal. (Example: I make $150,000 thousand per year, or I'm making $250,000 per year in 12 months.) Then follow the traditional steps, say it out loud, and go to the extreme by writing it down every day. It looks, sounds, and feels as if you are committed to that goal.

I have had the opportunity to sit in training and hear speakers talk about doing this more times than I would like to admit. But what they are *not* addressing is the strength of your personal internal belief. The strategy of saying it aloud every day might work for you, or you may never believe that it will happen. When it works, the person likely had an inner conviction about that goal.

Your belief in the goal is more important than reading it aloud or writing it down. If your brain does not believe the goal will ever happen, then every time you say it or read it, your brain will tell you why it's not true. The result is that it won't happen. Now that's a lot of counterproductive effort that will cause frustration and discouragement.

How can you acknowledge and increase your core beliefs?

Do you need to lower your goals to get closer to your belief level for a short time?

What is possible for you to achieve or attain?

You can keep your Big Hairy Audacious Goal (BHAG) and set smaller, more manageable goals that you believe are possible right now. Start with an attainable goal that will foster increased belief in yourself and your goal setting. Every time you set a goal and achieve it, you create a habit of achieving and believing yourself. According to Brian Tracy, you can get addicted to the emotional boost that you receive from accomplishing goals that you set.

Expand your vision as your belief system grows. Honor yourself with acceptance of where you are in this space.

Example:

If, in your mind, you see you and your spouse working at your current jobs until you retire, living out retirement in the same house you live in now, and driving your same gold Ford Taurus to bowling league every week, does that viewpoint support your goal of making one million dollars every year? Right now, the answer is likely a resounding, "Absolutely not!" Why do you think that is? Is it because it is not possible for you? Again, the answer is a resounding, "Absolutely not!"

Nothing will change without intentional effort on your part. Believe there is more for yourself than what you are doing today. Desire more for yourself.

You can change the trajectory of your life, and you need to believe it is possible. If your subconscious mind doesn't believe it will happen, though, you can take steps to be aware of the difference and make choices that change it.

If you say that your life is fine and you don't want anything to be different, you may be lowering your standards or disassociating with what you truly want. I bet it sounds silly that anyone would do that. In reality, it is a common way of coping with a potential loss. Did you catch that? It is a way to diminish the possibility of not achieving what you desire. It is all right to lower your goals and expectations to make them believable to work yourself back up to higher goals. On the other hand, it is an excuse to say that you don't want something to avoid encountering fear, loss, or disappointment.

What if you envision your kids and grandkids coming to your house, your current dining room, every Sunday for dinner? If you make one million dollars in the next twelve months, will that likely change your existing home or your plans for traveling during retirement? Will that work against your current vision for your future? Of course! So now your subconscious mind has to work against the goal you write down and say every day to protect your future.

That's right. Your mind is balancing itself out because you are trying to force it to think something, and it is forcing your actions to go back to the place you have already been. Here you sit, in mediocrity, without getting any results, and you become negative and frustrated. If you told others about this, you would now have to endure jabs and ridicule from your friends and loved ones. Worst of all, you start believing the goal doesn't work.

Even if you have some small successes in this situation, your subconscious mind will automatically bring you back to your place of safety and comfort. Your brain will create the circumstances necessary to create the future you see and believe in your subconscious mind. That fear of success or fear of failure you think you have may just be your mind doing its job. So how do you fix it?

Find out exactly what you want.

Suppose what you find through this exercise is disappointing, and you decide you want something more or different in your life. In that case, we will address how to internalize or emotionalize what you wish for in another section. If what you want is not believable to you, we will address that also.

The most important thing right now is to figure out what is in your subconscious mind and what motivates you to act. This is a very important step, so don't cut any corners. Your brain is so powerful. Your mind strives to work on shortcuts to work as quickly and efficiently as possible. We all have beliefs about ourselves that came from our childhood experiences. They can go unnoticed by us without realizing what those beliefs are or how they are shaping our everyday decisions and choices. Your thoughts can dictate everything you do. Do you want to let those beliefs control your life, or do you want to be in control?

Next, you will learn how to find out what has been driving your belief system so you can decide what changes you want to make.

Start with the End in Mind

Sit quietly in a relaxed position with your journal and writing instrument available. Here is the first step toward the future you always wanted to live, so try to limit interruptions during this process. Get a preprinted journal at margospilde.com/resources.

Ten Simple Steps to Prioritize Your Next Thirty Years

Day One

Imagine yourself and your family thirty years into the future. How old will you be? How old will your kids and spouse be? Write down the ages for a reference point. As a side note, if thirty years from now feels too long, please start with twenty years. It would help if you didn't have mental energy spent on visions of an old folks' home.

Where do you live? How does your life look? What do you do with your time? Where are your kids and spouse? Who is around you? Where do you spend your time every day?

Write this in your journal.

Day One—Twenty-four-hour question: What do I want to be doing in thirty years?

Now close your eyes and think about it. Write down everything that comes to mind. Write down anything that pops into your mind through the next day and possibly even longer. Your brain will answer the questions that you ask it. (The questions that our parents put into our brains as children are seldom useful.) That is one of the reasons why speaking well to yourself is so important.

Most people have never thought about this before, and things won't immediately come to mind. The most effective way to get true answers is to let your subconscious mind work on this for twenty-four hours. After you have written down everything that comes to mind, repeat the question to yourself several times, close your journal, and do something else.

Your subconscious mind will answer the question you have asked while doing your daily activities. It will also help to review your entries at least once throughout the day and before you go to bed. Immediately before going to bed, read your twenty-four-hour question and let your subconscious mind work on it while you sleep. Make sure you review today's exercise before going on with tomorrow's exercise. That may remind you of things that popped up, and you did not remember to write down.

*** Doing all of these exercises in one sitting may work better for you. You will see results either way. Make sure you give your brain time to ponder the questions. Write down all thoughts that come to mind because those often are often the most important for your future. ***

Day Two

Get out your journal and read your entries from Day One.

After reviewing what you wrote for Day One, answer some of these questions. Let your desires take over. You have allowed your dreams to be locked away for too long. Let them out of the vault, and they will get a life of their own.

- What color and style is your house?
- Is it the one you WANT to live in for the rest of your life?
- Where is your house?
- What do you do with your time?
- Are you golfing, flying, traveling, fishing, racing?
- Are you living on a beach, mountain, ocean, lake, or river?

Write down your answers and all the cool things that your mind leads you to discover. If what you wrote down is to the extreme, congratulations. I have a lot of faith in you and your success.

You probably don't have enough detail to manifest this into your life yet. It will come. Your extreme dreams will illicit wonderful and exciting details that you haven't thought about previously.

Your dreams can motivate you to do things that you never thought possible. The bigger, the better.

If what you wrote down is barely above your current lifestyle, you are manifesting a "just-get-by" mentality or don't believe anything else is possible for you. In both of those scenarios, you have the choice to change your belief (as we discussed previously), and you have permission to think bigger and dream bigger. Take this as your first step, and begin to build bigger dreams that will take you further than you ever thought was possible.

Write the following statement in your journal.

Day Two—Twenty-four-hour question: What do I REALLY want to be doing in thirty years?

Now close your eyes and think about it. Be very specific with the details of your life. Build upon what you wrote down yesterday.

After you have written down everything that comes to mind, repeat the question to yourself several times, close your journal, and do something else. Just as yesterday, review your entries at least once during the day and before bedtime. Immediately before going to bed, read your twenty-four-hour question and let your mind work on it while you sleep. Make sure you review today's exercise before going on with tomorrow's exercise so that you can remember and write down what your brain came up with and that you may have forgotten to write down.

Day Three

In the last twenty-four hours, you should have taken the rubber band off your brain and let your dreams take hold. Do you feel more energized and alive than you have felt for a long time? Maybe you have more bounce in your step. Do you catch yourself smiling more often and feel just a little happier?

Keep feeling these positive thoughts and emotions. You will now build upon the mental pictures you have created of your future.

Pick one item out of your journal from chapter two that gives you the happiest feelings. It can be anything you want, whether it is practical or not. It's practice. Make it fun. You might choose to play eighteen holes of golf every day, go skydiving, or sit next to your infinity-edge pool every day while Javier brings you mai tais on demand.

After choosing one, write the following statement in your journal and use the item you selected in the blank.

Day Three—Twenty-four-hour question: How will I feel when I am _____?

Envision being in that place. Write down how you feel. What is the sensation in your body? Where are you feeling it? You want to notice and name the feelings; be very specific. You are truly living this right now because your brain does not differentiate between practicing for real and practicing in your mind. Research has proven this when scientists studied athletes and musicians. Your brain does not know the difference between being physically in a situation or living it in your mind.

Close your eyes and see yourself in this situation. Live this in your mind. Who is there with you? How do you feel? Is it hot or cold? Are you feeling wind or warmth? After you have felt and lived your future in your mind, write down how you felt in your journal using descriptive words.

Next, move on to another item in your journal. Make sure you have truly felt the first one before you move on. Some people will have an easier time seeing this in their lives and feeling the emotions than others. It's a learned skill and takes practice to master. Take your time. Try out different locations and times of day to see if that helps.

Day Four

Make sure to get your emotions involved before moving on to more steps.

For much of my life, I spent time reading books with steps that were sure to give me what I wanted, and I didn't experience many results. My life was not changed or impacted. That's why I wrote this book. Everyone can change one's own circumstances and live a life of thriving. There isn't a cookie-cutter approach that works for everyone. Pursue it intentionally.

We are all in different places in our lives. We all need a slightly different push to get where we want to go. As it was for me, the difference for you may be simply be not giving up. I kept going and kept looking, despite my frustration. I am certain you will see results by following these steps and emotionalizing them in your life. The only way you can fail is by not participating.

Let's start to move things up a bit in the timeline and envision your life closer to the present.

Write the following statement in your journal.

Day Four—Twenty-four-hour question: What does my life look like in twenty years? (If you started with twenty, go to fifteen years next.)

Build upon your previous entries. Write down your age and your spouse's and kids' ages. Write what you truly want, not what you think can actually happen for you within your lifetime. These are important exercises, and there is no right or wrong answer. Let the picture in your mind take hold and grow with it.

Day Five

Congratulations on getting this far. If you are reading this, I know you are participating with your heart and yearning and striving for change in your life.

You guessed it. Ten years (or five years) will be next. I hope you aren't jumping ahead. Allow your brain to have time to come up with answers to the questions you are asking. Your mind is powerful, and the emotions you create will drive your desires.

Your deepest desires are powerful motivators for action. You have hopes, dreams, wants, and a few ideas that you have never said aloud to anyone. The plans you hold in your heart will not become a reality without a deep desire at your core. Your wishes come with emotions.

If you have been speeding through the exercises the way I would, take time to go back and emotionalize what you want in your life. Pausing to reflect on what you desire and creating the emotion around what you want is most important. I am proud of your commitment. Changes will be happening for the better in your life.

Write the following statement in your journal.

Day Five—Twenty-four-hour question: What does my life look like in ten years? (If you started with twenty, go to five years next.)

Again, work backward from your previous journal entries. Write down your age and the ages of your spouse and kids. I can't stress how much more real this makes the exercise feel and how it will impact your thoughts.

Is this one a little scary? If you are like me, you know ten years will go by seemingly in an instant. Take some extra time with this one because your mind will be struggling with what you want from the previous questions and what it feels is possible to accomplish this quickly.

Ten years is not far away. You will tend to be more conservative with your dreams and goals at this step. Look at what you wanted thirty years into the future and set ten-year goals based on that lifestyle. Eventually, you will see how to make this happen for yourself in the follow-up action steps, but for now, keep your dreams flowing. You will probably feel discouraged and believe these goals are unattainable, just stick with it. You want your life to change, don't you? You have to think big to change big.

Day Six

Previously I mentioned that you might feel discouraged about attaining this new life in ten short years. Discouragement can keep you where you are, or you can work through it and enjoy your life of abundance. *You will always get what you expect.* Awareness of what you want and what is holding you back is crucial. Today, you will take a moment to see and feel what is limiting your belief in attaining your dream life.

Today, you will have two steps in the process. *Please do not stop with the first step.* What you focus on grows, and creating the alternate belief is the most important step in awareness. If you do not change your alternate state of thinking, you will give your old belief system more power. You can be in control. You are strong enough to follow through and not let it stop you again.

Write the following statement in your journal on the left side of the page.

Day Six, Part 1—First twenty-four-hour question: What is limiting my thinking right now?

Use a list format down the left side of the paper for your answers, one item per line. Make sure you write only on the left half of the paper. You will be using the right half for the second part of this exercise.

After you have written down and exhausted everything you can think of for what is limiting your thinking, write the next question below. Follow the same process and answer that question until all your reasons have been exhausted.

Day Six, Part 1—Second twenty-four-hour question: What don't I believe will happen for me?

Follow the same format as above for both the second and third questions. Answer all three questions until all your reasons have been exhausted.

Day Six, Part 1—Third twenty-four-hour question: Why don't I believe it can or will happen for me?

After you have finished with all the reasons and excuses of why you can't do what you want, you will move on to the reasons you can.

Write the following statement in your journal <u>on the right side of the page</u>.

Day Six, Part 2—Twenty-four-hour question: What is the opposing way to think about this statement that will give me the power to move forward?

Take this opportunity to write an opposing statement for every limiting belief and excuse that you wrote down previously. What is the opposite way to think or believe about that statement that gives you the power to move forward?

You may have more limiting beliefs come to mind than you imagined were possible. Maybe there are so many that you didn't write them all down. Take the time to write down anything that comes to mind during this exercise. Often the opposing reasons that seem the most comfortable are the biggest obstacles holding you back. Maybe you have accepted them as not possible for you. Those thoughts seem normal because you have lived with them for such a long time. If it pops into your mind, it is holding you back. For me, I did not want to speak anywhere, even in small groups. It was a habit for me, and I felt comfortable being someone who doesn't talk. The problem was that it was holding me back, and I had no intention of doing anything to change it.

Day Seven

Have you been taking the exercises seriously up to today? I hope so because it keeps getting tougher to believe that major changes are possible the closer you get to the present moment.

You are now going to look at five years into the future. (You can choose one, two, or three years out if you are an older adult.) As you know, five years will fly by in an instant. Unfortunately, you may not be living your life to the fullest. If you let your life continue to run its course without any intention toward changing, you may never make any changes.

The movie *Click* with Adam Sandler was a great wakeup call for me to decide to do something different in my life so I could have different results. We all tend to go into autopilot mode when difficult times show up. We want to fast forward through the tough times. Often, you won't see what is missing in your life or what you can do differently to live a more abundant life. I hope a sense of aliveness and joy for yourself emerges. I pray that you start living your life on purpose rather than on autopilot.

Write the following statement in your journal.

Day Seven—Twenty-four-hour question: How will my life be different from today, five years from this moment?

Work backward from your ten-year entry to avoid the pitfall of being too conservative in your desires and life changes because of the short time frame. At this point, your brain may start saying, "Oh no, that's not possible," or "It would help to lower that slightly; it's only five years from now."

Maybe you're wondering, "How can I ever achieve that in the next five years?" It's OK if you are thinking, "We don't have any money, we have two kids to feed, and last week the washing machine started making a noise," but don't let those limiting beliefs and your current reality stop you from dreaming. Nothing will ever change if you allow those thoughts to continue affecting the choices and decisions in your life.

Day Eight

Now is when you pull everything together and give your dreams more focus and clarity.

CALL TO ACTION

Get a second journal and ask your spouse to go through these exercises independently.

- It will foster communication and excitement in your marriage.
- Plan a date night for the two of you to get together to talk about what you have both written down.

It will be a fun date night full of dreaming and wishes. I bet you haven't had a night with your spouse with that much energy and excitement for years.

Write the following statement in your journal.

Day Eight—Twenty-four-hour question: What steps do I need to take to reach _____?

Use each item you wrote down from Day Seven to fill in the blanks for this question. You will do each one individually. Write down every step you can think of that will be needed to achieve your result. Make certain you have exhausted every possible step before going on to the next item. If something comes to mind for a previous item after you have moved on, write it down.

There will be no particular order to these steps as you start writing. It is brainstorming, and you don't want to stop and dwell on anything or think about how much work or effort a step may take. Keep writing down everything that comes to mind and anything you might need to accomplish each goal.

This exercise is an emotional roller coaster. At first, you will feel great because you are accomplishing so much by writing down these steps. Then suddenly, you might feel overwhelmed with all the steps involved. Just **keep writing**. Push through the negative feelings, walk away if you need a break, and keep coming back until your list is complete. This step is very important to your success.

Day Nine

Are you feeling a little overwhelmed or maybe even exhausted from thinking about everything you need to do? Don't worry; if I told you to get out there and make it happen at this point, you would probably never accomplish it. We'll work through the steps together to get to the action part.

Write the following statement in your journal.

Day Nine—Twenty-four-hour question: What is the one item that must be accomplished FIRST to reach my goals?

You may feel there is more than one answer for number one, or you can't decide which one should be first. That's all right; it will all work itself out. Pick one, and you can always change it later. Now is where you will simplify all of those tasks and prioritize.

Was it clear to you where you should start? When you look at your list, logically, there should be a general area that is obvious to start. There may be multiple items that seem to be first. As I said earlier, choose one, and if you realize that you need to change it later, be flexible and move forward.

The main point is that you don't want to start your list by picking a piece of land before needing a building. There are many steps to creating a viable business. Don't skip early steps to do something that may sound more exciting. Once you look at the list, pick a starting point. It makes everything seem easier, and accomplishing the task will feel more achievable.

You are doing great to get this far. Put the rest of your items in a somewhat logical order. They will likely change order many times, so don't spend much time thinking about it. There may be many support steps that go along with each main task. Emphasize the primary mission and list secondary items with it. To get a good order for tasks, ask yourself these two questions: "What should be started soon or can be easily finalized?" and "What doesn't need much effort in the next two to three years and can still be accomplished by my five-year goal line?" These questions will give you an idea of how to rank everything.

Day Ten

Day Ten—Action Step 1: Read the goal, dreams, and desires you created.

A little progress each day adds up to BIG results.

Day Ten—Action Step 2: Do something today toward your five-year goal.

Make a habit of doing something every day toward your goal. It can be big or small. You will create new patterns and place your goal in your mind every day. Take action now, rather than closing your journal and not reading it again for seven months.

I have often made goals and never thought about them again. It's time to create a new habit.

I prefer to write out my to-do list the night before. Some people do it every day before leaving for work. Choose the best solution for you and take a few moments to think about tomorrow. With the short time invested in planning, you will become laser-focused on your goals and tasks.

Every day, add one thing from your big list that you can do on your lunch hour, before walking to a meeting, or first thing in the morning. You can even set the alarm on your phone to alert you every day to do that one thing.

Take baby steps and think about your goals. Do something every day toward your goal. In Brian Tracy's book, *Eat That Frog*, he said you can develop a "positive addiction" to the endorphins released from finishing tasks, leading to you become addicted to success and contribution.

Wouldn't you like to be addicted to accomplishing tasks? If you google that idea, you will find that many people believe it to be true. I am unclear if the science behind it will stand up to the medical professional's test. Either way, I want to experience an addiction to success. The idea behind this is that you will feel a sense of energy and enthusiasm as you accomplish an important task. Completing tasks will trigger the release of endorphins in your brain, and those endorphins will cause you to feel a natural high. As you continue to complete challenging and important tasks, you will become addicted to the feeling that you get from the endorphins. It sounds a lot like a runner's high. I have never gotten any good feelings from running, but it seems that many people do.

5

Live Your Life on Purpose

"For I know the plans I have for you," declares the LORD,
"plans to prosper you and not to harm you,
plans to give you hope and a future."
(Jeremiah 29:11, NIV)

COMPLETING THE EXERCISES in previous chapters will clarify your direction and purpose in three ways:

1. What you like versus what you don't like.
2. What you want versus what you don't want in life.
3. What you believe your future should look like versus the direction it is currently moving.

It will bring awareness to areas of your life that are often ignored and focus your thoughts on what you want to achieve. Awareness enables you to pinpoint the direction you should be going and your passion and purpose in life.

After doing these exercises, you will likely have a major definite direction or aim where you desire to go. The steps give you a good idea of where to begin. Congratulations on coming so far on your journey. I am excited for you.

If you have done well with the exercises but have only a vague sense of what direction you should go, that is excellent progress. Imagine how much further along you are on your journey after this short time. It often takes a long time to figure out where you are going in life, and the journey is all about learning while you try different avenues. Every step forward brings you closer to knowing your purpose and calling in life.

If you are still searching for your purpose, give yourself some grace. You may not have given this subject much thought previously, and your brain hasn't formed the new neural pathways it needs to provide you with an answer yet. Allow the time for your subconscious mind to process all the information it has received. You will be surprised how quickly your brain begins to generate new ideas and answers after being given some time to process. Be creative and think about the many ways you provide value to others. The world is abundant with infinite opportunities, and there is a unique way that works just for you.

The next exercise will help you connect to the purpose you have in your heart and develop the passion you need to accomplish it. Once you have a deep sense of what you feel inside of you, the focus will soon follow, and your passion will be the driving force.

Emotionalize

The next exercise will be to emotionalize your goals and dreams. We all say we want certain things, but do we want them enough to put the work into achieving them? You want to experience the emotion of having what you desire, so it feels real to you.

Sometimes you want something, but you don't recognize the underlying reason why you want it. There could be a need inside of you that has been unmet, and you want something that meets that need for you in the short term. This scenario is similar to an addiction, where it meets a need the person has and gives him an emotional boost without fixing the underlying need. When you are "medicating" a wound in your heart with personal possessions or responses from others, it will always leave you feeling empty soon after.

Use this tool to discover **why** you want some of what you wrote down from the last chapter. It will help you understand your motivation and pinpoint what you truly want for yourself.

Fill in the first blank with your goal or desire:

"I want _____ because getting this will make me feel _____ and will give me _____."

Examples:

I want to make $100,000 per year because getting this will make me feel important and will give me more respect.

I want to buy rental houses because getting this will make me feel rich and will give me more friends.

I want to learn real estate investing because getting this will make me feel confident and knowledgeable and will give me the opportunity to create a legacy for my family the way wealthy people do.

I want to travel because getting this will make me feel happy and will give me more stories to share.

What is driving you to achieve? In the first example above, it was eye opening to understand my underlying reason for making $100,000. People were telling me that my goal should be to earn $100,000, and my drive to reach it was to earn respect within the group and to have more friends. In that example, it's easy to see why I wasn't motivated to make money. I desired trust, respect, and friendship more than money.

Once you know your driving force, you can re-evaluate if it is a healthy drive or if you need to look at your internal feelings. In the first example, I realized that I wanted to feel important, to be respected, and to have more friends. It did not keep me motivated to work hard, only to continue receiving validation from others because the confirmation of my worth was over quickly.

What do you truly desire? Evaluate your true desires and authentic motivation underlying what you think you want. This exercise will show your truest desires and set you on the best path toward what you want. When I understood my true need, it gave me the freedom to work toward other goals, and it became easier to find my purpose in this world. Finding my core emotion was key to making it possible, and you can do the same.

Direction, Desire, and Discipline

There are three steps you need to live your life on purpose:

- Direction
- Desire
- Discipline

The little things you do intentionally will turn into habits, and eventually they will give you great results. Your results will be directly proportional to what you think, what you earnestly desire, and what you put into practice with your daily habits.

> *Shoot for the moon. Even if you miss,*
> *you'll land among the stars.*
> (Norman Vincent Peale)

When you aim for the moon, you will tap into and create a direct link to your desire. You probably had the desire already. It may be buried under layers of disbelief and years of non-activity. Life gets in the way, and we sometimes forget to focus on the dreams and desires of our youth. The more mature adults in our lives can drive those wild thoughts right out of us and tell us how we should be thinking and acting. It's all right to think up wild and crazy ideas again.

Now, your deepest desires have come to the surface. The only job left is to put your new disciplines in place. Discipline is where we always get stuck, isn't it? I know how to lose weight and eat healthily. It's easier to stay home than work out, and I would much prefer to grab a bite to eat on the way home than stop at the grocery store to buy vegetables that must be cleaned and chopped. It is always easier to do what you have always done than to create new ways of being.

Successful people have successful habits. Unsuccessful people have unsuccessful habits. If you are not getting what you want in life, you may not have implemented successful practices. Great news! It is easy to implement new patterns with a little information and structure.

CALL TO ACTION

Practice this with your spouse and your kids.

I want _____ because getting that will make me feel _____ and will give me more _____.

Example: I want __to wear my boyfriend's shirt___ because getting that will make me feel __loved and will give me more ___people who acknowledge me____.

What is the difference between someone who decides to lose his excess weight and successfully does so and someone who says he wants to lose weight but can't? The person who lost the weight finally *felt* what it would be like to lose forty pounds. He could *see* himself living life without the extra weight, and he *believed* he could do it and became motivated to do what was necessary. After seeing the results in his mind and feeling the achievement's emotions, he **created new successful habits.** The key to being intentional and following through on new habits is setting yourself up for success and believing it is possible. Create a new pattern of following through on commitments to yourself and collecting wins.

Key point: Start with small goals that you can achieve rather effortlessly and make certain you achieve them.

Everything you do is a result of your emotions, which guide your beliefs. Make sure you give yourself a new habit that is believable and achievable. How you *feel* about something dictates whether you **believe** it and subsequently whether you can **see** it happening in your life.

- **Feel It:** Emotionalize it for yourself
- **See It:** Visualize it in your life
- **Believe It:** Trust that it is possible

Figure out why you want something. Once you believe it, set up a structure to do it, and the discipline will happen more easily. It is no longer straight willpower or effort to make yourself do what it takes to achieve that goal in your life. You will do whatever you need to do to achieve the desired outcome because that is what you truly want to be doing.

Discipline Strategies

Even with a burning desire to accomplish your goal, you will still need to implement some discipline strategies in your life. The tendency to continue doing what you have always done will be stronger than your newly realized desire. The twenty-one-day standard to create a new habit has been debunked. It takes as long as it takes for you. As you get older, it will take longer. It's not easy to change or eliminate three, four, or five decades of doing things the same way. When you continue to be intentional about your new success habits, they will eventually turn into great long-term success habits.

The new habits you create will improve every aspect of your life. It may even change your children's future success and alter the lives of future generations for your family. If you make way for your children and family to see what you are doing, they can participate in what you are learning. One of the many benefits of working on these disciplines for yourself is that you can teach your children simultaneously. People can achieve more success faster when they do not have to *un*-learn beforehand.

If you aren't certain where to begin, read through the following list of successful habits and pick one to start implementing in your life. Do not try to change everything at once because you will surely fail. Start with something that seems easy for you, and once you have mastered that as a new habit, look at tackling another new habit. Write the following statement in your journal; after reading through the following ideas, pick which discipline strategy you want to work on first and commit to it.

Write the following statement in your journal.

What new positive habits am I committed to achieving in my life?

Commit to ONE PER DAY MINIMUM

Commit to doing something every day to work toward your dreams and goals. Look at what you have already written in your journal and start with one of your goals.

Everyone is busy, and taking on a new project may be overwhelming. Do not let that stop you. Guilt, among other things, has a way of sneaking in and sabotaging your hopes and dreams. Commit to doing something every day toward your desired destination, no matter how small it might be. Set up a reminder on your phone, add it to your daily to-do list, you will eventually get there.

- **Become an Expert**

   Commit to spending thirty minutes **most days** learning, studying, or practicing in your chosen area, and you will eventually become an expert in that area. You could do this in your current field or choose a new field to learn. That process is how anyone begins to learn something new. It could be crypto, real estate, day trading, or buying notes. Many people waste at least thirty minutes a day scrolling on their phones, watching Netflix, playing games, or scanning social media. Use that time to your advantage. With a little focus, you could be well on your way to living the life you want to live.

   Even if you don't know about the direction you want to go or haven't started, commit to learning now. Begin with thirty minutes a day, and be intentional about it. Eventually, you will know the important stuff, and if you keep up the habit, you will become an expert.

- **Create Triggers**

   Create healthy triggers or reminders in your daily routine to practice your new beneficial habits. Using affirmation statements in the morning, reading your goals, or repeating your intention statements can become success habits built into your daily routine. Like most people, I do not do these things every day. Doing them sometimes will reap results bigger and more quickly than never doing them. Be kind to yourself and give yourself grace.

   Speak words of success rather than words of defeat to yourself. Build the associations into your day that create a reminder or trigger to do the tasks you want to implement. That intention will help you remember more often and continue your new trajectory toward successful habits.

It's important to collect wins rather than losses. If you can reward yourself with small wins, it will keep you moving toward your goals. It takes much more than twenty-one days to create a new habit. What do you love doing, and how can you use that to reward yourself for doing the things you don't want to do? Give yourself grace and room to make mistakes, so you aren't too hard on yourself.

What can you do while waiting for your coffee in the morning? I like to put notes and reminders near my coffee pot to see them first. You could post notes on your mirror in the bathroom or by your toothbrush. Time alone in the shower can be a powerful and useful time in your day. Here are some examples of triggers or reminders in your daily life.

I went to a T. Harv Eker seminar many years ago based on his book *Secrets of the Millionaire Mind*. He suggested doing movements while you repeat your affirmations because it helps you learn them through associative learning. It does get my blood pumping and wakes me up quickly, so I'm ready to go in the morning. I also heard a very successful person say he always did his affirmations in the shower. Be creative. It can be fun.

- **Pattern Interrupt**

  When you begin to think of a negative thought that inhibits your success in any area, say, "STOP." Say it to yourself or preferably out loud to interrupt your current thought process. It is also helpful to clap once loudly as you say it. That will create an increased learning association opportunity.

  Use the word "STOP" rather than "No" because if you start staying "No" to something, you are giving the thought more power rather than eliminating the power of that negative thought. You may be giving it more power by increasing the emotion or passion toward that thought.

  Saying, "No, I don't want to think about failure in this project" will keep you focused on the word "failure" as your brain eliminates the word "no" at the front of your statement. Have you ever heard the analogy about telling yourself not to think about red cars or pink elephants? When you tell yourself not to do something, your brain will skip over the "no" and focus on the subject.

Another example of this is when you buy a new car. You will start seeing that car in the same color everywhere. When you tell yourself, "No, stop looking at them," it won't stop you from seeing them. We had this happen when my daughter was a new driver. We did not want to spend much money on another car, and she had several interesting ideas of what she wanted to drive. While looking at car lots, she spotted a black Cadillac SRX. It had over 100,000 miles, was physically in great shape both inside and outside, and was in our price range. Suddenly, our family saw black Cadillac SRXs everywhere. I can honestly say I had never noticed that car in my lifetime, and it became annoying to have them pointed out with alarming frequency. It did not help telling my kids or my husband, "Don't point those out anymore." They just kept seeing them. People had been driving those Cadillacs around town before we bought one, so why hadn't I noticed them before?

When you use "no" or "don't," you think more about failure. If you use "STOP," then pause, tell your brain to stop, and interrupt the thought, you will then have time to pause as your brain begins to follow your command.

- **Rewrite and Replace**

  Replace the negative thought with a more productive one. There are three ways in which you may create a more positive outlook:

  1. Replace your thought with a positive affirmation or goal statement.

Let's say you are starting a business in real estate. One of your affirmations could be, "I have ten properties rented at one hundred percent capacity." Imagine how your life would change if you made that statement every time you thought negatively. This statement likely has nothing to do with your current negativity. All you are doing is training your brain to be thinking in the direction you want it to go. You will surely be more focused on your goal if you think about it more frequently throughout the day.

2. Pick a catchphrase you use all the time to replace your negative thoughts.

A catchphrase could have to do with any topic. It creates a new belief for yourself or reinforces your existing belief system. When you replace negative thoughts with this new phrase, you will continuously work on your new belief system throughout the day. Some examples:

- Money comes easily and frequently to me.
- Every day I get better and better.
- I am getting better every day.
- I am the luckiest person I know.
- Luck is when preparation meets opportunity.
- Everything I touch turns to gold.
- I am the happiest person I know.
- I have plenty of time to get everything done.
- I have plenty of money to buy everything I need.

Do you see how creating your catchphrase could be extremely beneficial? If there is a certain area where you need to get better, design a phrase for yourself that describes what you want and repeat it frequently. You can also change or add new ones to your life as your phrase becomes internalized for you.

I was always running late and felt frazzled. When my then two-year-old started to gripe at me to hurry so we wouldn't be late, I realized something needed to be changed. The phrase that I was constantly repeating in my mind was, "There's never enough time to get everything done." Previously, I hadn't noticed myself thinking that. It was a habit I didn't know I had. After seeing my pattern, I replaced the thought of never having enough time with a new phrase: "I have plenty of time to get everything done." It didn't take long before the detrimental thought was gone from my mind, and I started to be late less often. Sometimes I was even on time, and the most important change was that I no longer yelled at my daughter to hurry up so we could get out of the house.

Money and negative thought patterns are common. Most people don't even realize they have them. What do you think about when you have to pay a bill or buy something? Do you think, "There is never enough money"? If you believe this statement or a similar phrase, do you think you will ever live a life where you have plenty of money? It's not possible, is it? That is because your controlling belief is that there is never enough money. Your subconscience will ensure your life matches your belief system, so even if more money shows up, you will spend it somewhere to match your reality to your belief.

Listen to yourself for the phrases that frequently come to mind. Consciously draft new ones for yourself. I have often used the phrase, "There is never enough money." No matter how much money we had, I was mentally creating a scarcity because we had to buy this and pay for that. There seemed never to be enough. Now I intentionally repeat the phrases, "There's plenty of money" and "I find money everywhere I go." When you replace your thoughts, watch how your beliefs will change.

3. Flip your negative thought into the positive form.

This habit takes more thought and effort because you have to recognize the negative thinking first, then think about it, and turn the thought into a positive statement. It can create results more quickly because of the effort and awareness involved. You are forcing yourself to change every negative thought into the opposite positive form, which puts more emotion behind your thoughts.

EXAMPLE: Suppose you wanted to start a car wash business, and you were having trouble finding a good location at a good price. You may think to yourself, "This is impossible. I will never find anything that works." In this situation, rather than repeating your catchphrase, turn your negative thought into a positive phrase that will help you attain your goal: "I am quickly and easily finding the best possible location for my car wash, and I am having fun doing it." (If you put the word "fun" into every statement, life will be a lot more enjoyable.)

Pick a strategy and use it consistently to make it a new habit. Once you become good at one of these habits, begin to work on another one to magnify your results. It should never be a time-consuming task to monitor your thoughts. A little bit of intention will bring big results. You are simply replacing the non-productive habits you learned in childhood with new patterns that will be more beneficial.

Think about how much advantage you are giving your children when you teach them how to think positively now. You are providing them with this tool when they are young, and they will not have to unlearn as many bad habits as adults. Nothing will stop them from accomplishing what they want to do in this world. Just give them a chance and some useful tools.

- **Have an Attitude of Gratitude**

Live a life of gratitude and awe. Be thankful for everything you have in your life right now. Be grateful for the good and the mediocre and even the not-so-good things in your life. Be thankful for the things that you take for granted and that you may not always enjoy or appreciate in your life. I can grumble about how many spoons and cereal bowls have piled up on the counter again today, or I can intentionally choose to thank God for healthy, happy children who get food for themselves when they are hungry.

Wake up every morning and be thankful for all you have and all you are. You can write in your planner, create a note on your phone, or just give thanks in prayer. Anything that reminds you to be thankful will work. If you are naturally inclined toward gratefulness, that's wonderful. Most of us are not and have not seen that modeled. Being intentionally grateful is an excellent way to learn a new skill and habit that brings you abundant joy.

Appreciate and be in awe of everything around you. Your life and surroundings are wonderful blessings. It is impossible to have negative or discouraging thoughts and be thankful simultaneously. For many people, giving thanks or saying "thank you" means they are saying it to God. If you are a Christian, absolutely make God the focus of everything you are doing here. Ask for guidance and give thanks to Him.

Many speakers and trainers will say to thank the universe. I have heard plenty of Christians say they are against listening to their shared information solely because of that.

Speakers and trainers don't want to offend non-Christians, and they don't want to limit themselves by promoting to only Christians.

Have grace for others who are doing their best in the world the same way you are motivated to do your best. It is all right to give them a break. Don't use it as an excuse not to make changes for yourself. When you have an open mind, you will see much of the material is similar to or based on biblical laws and principles.

You don't have to be a Christian to use them, and they will work for anyone who implements them. If you are not a believer in God, be thankful to the universe wherever you feel comfortable. I urge you to keep an open mind that there may be a God out there working in your favor, and it's acceptable that we all have different beliefs.

- **Become a Great Receiver**

   Be open to receiving and becoming a gracious receiver. Many good things flow to you all the time. To receive anything, you must be available to receive it and willing to accept it. Be open to accepting all the good things that come your way.

   If you are offered a gift and do not accept it, you will not receive it. When you receive another chance to receive a gift, will you be available to accept it the second time? Availability and willingness to receive include blessings, compliments, gifts, help, assistance, or anything that someone is willing to give you without expecting something in return.

   Notice how people respond when they receive a gift or a compliment. Did they receive it well, or did their response unconsciously tell the giver they are unworthy to accept or receive what was offered?

   There are many ways that people unconsciously project their inability to receive a gift or blessing on others. Take note of ways you don't receive well and work toward responding differently:

- Projecting your ability on others: You turn away a gift because you have nothing or could never give that gift to another person although you don't know that person's situation or heart.
- Batting away or deflecting: You respond by making a joke or sarcastic comment. Frequently people do this with compliments. It diminishes the person giving the praise, and he will eventually learn not to bother offering compliments.
- Refusing gifts: Sometimes people will refuse gifts that could greatly improve their lives. They say "no" or "no thank you" because they don't feel worthy of the gifts.

When you turn down a gift that you don't feel worthy of receiving, you limit blessings and abundance in your life. Offers, blessings, and gifts will eventually stop coming when you continue to turn them down. How are you blocking the possibility of "more" in your life? It is difficult to be blessed when you say, "No, I don't need it or want it." Make a point to alter your internal dialogue from "I don't deserve this" to "I'm thankful you gave this to me."

When somebody offers you words of encouragement, compliments, advice, wisdom, help, food, clothing, gifts of any kind, or time, respond with an open upward-facing palm, and say, "Thank you."

- **Recognize the Possibilities**
  Look for the good in every situation. When you look for bad things to happen, many good things will go unnoticed and unaccepted. If you want to experience more good in your life, look for the good in everything.

EXAMPLE: You are driving, and a rock flies at you and smashes your windshield. What is your typical reaction? Would you get angry, start yelling, and maybe even run down the person who threw up the rock to give him a piece of your mind? Would that incident ruin the rest of your day? A better way to respond is, "That is not great, but at least nobody was hurt" or "This must have happened for a reason; I wonder what that reason could be."

What if a diversion or minor event postponed you from being somewhere else that would have caused more harm to you? Anything that shifts your current focus may be bringing you to something else you need in your life or away from something you don't. Often you will not know the exact reason why something happened. When your heart and mind are open to finding a cause and looking for the good in all situations, you will see great things happening more often.

We had a contractor who came to fix a problem that arose from the poor work of a previous contractor. The original problem became worse with everything the new contractor did to repair a badly leaking shower. Water would run directly into the drywall in the basement ceiling. I could have gotten extremely angry and hateful. It would have been easy to justify that we were wronged by two different people who should know how to build a shower to contain water.

The water problem took out an entire room in our basement. Twice. The second contractor called me immediately after looking at the project in this scenario. He said, "Do you know your roof has hail damage? You should call your insurance company." His motivation was personal because he wanted to get the job of installing a new $20,000 roof. I did call my insurance company, and it turned out he was right. I got a new roof and fabulous six-inch gutters, which we desperately needed. All we paid was the cost of our deductible plus the upcharge from five- to six-inch gutters. It was such a blessing to have all of that work for a minimal amount of money.

My choice was to focus on the over $20,000 blessing we received. At that time, nobody else had hail damage in our neighborhood. One close neighbor called, but their insurance company said their roof had no damage. It was a gift orchestrated by God that I could not ignore. I hired a reputable company to install the roof and refused to pay the contractor for the shower that did not hold water. Rather than being down on myself and asking how I could have been so stupid, it became an experience that I will remember as a gift and a bigger blessing than I could have ever imagined.

Believing this situation was a gift and blessing may sound absurd. Open yourself to new ideas and perspectives. You might begin to see an unlikely scenario become a blessing disguised as an obstacle.

- **Believe in the Good**

    Believe that good things will happen to you. Good can happen FOR you and TO you. An important discipline is to believe that **it is** possible for you to live the life of abundance that you desire. It is possible that good things will happen for you in all circumstances.

    Going through the steps in the previous chapters will help you figure out what you truly want in life and foster a spark of belief in your heart and mind. You have talents, skills, and abilities that no one else on earth has. Even if you have similar skills and talents as someone else, you are the only person with the exact combination of everything you need to deliver the precise way you can provide it. *You are the only person who can do what you are doing.* Unfortunately, many of us put disbelief in front of our eyes so that we lose sight of what truly is possible.

    You can do everything. I intend to work to instill this in my children. I desire them to grow up believing they can do anything and everything they decide to do. Isn't it time you instill that belief in your own mind?

- **Become a Dreamer**

  Create a dream board or vision board. You can do this with a giant poster board, file folder, or anything available. Choose pictures to hang on your mirror or wall. Create a digital slideshow on your phone, iPad, or laptop. The primary objective is to take intangible thoughts in your head and turn them into tangible items that you can see. Dream boards help you remember what you want and allow your brain an opportunity to work on achieving those dreams subconsciously. Your dreams can become a reality when you see what you want to accomplish. Having a real picture in front of you hastens the truth in your mind.

  Almost fifteen years ago, my husband said he wanted a Ford Mustang. His favorite was the blue one with two thick white stripes on the hood. We had a young child and I did not work any longer. He was in the middle of his surgery training, and we did not have extra money to buy a car. When I was paging through a magazine, I came across a full-page ad picturing a blue mustang with two thick white stripes. I tore out the picture and hung it up on the wall in our bedroom above his dresser. He commented on the photo when he got home from work the next day. I had already forgotten about it.

  We went on with our lives, and one day my husband mentioned the magazine picture on the wall. After walking by that picture multiple times a day, we had that exact car in our driveway without realizing it. I had never given it a thought. It was quite amazing to see how we had brought exactly what we wanted into our lives. Unfortunately, Mark Wahlberg hasn't manifested in my life yet. One of his underwear ads hung in my closet for at least six years. There is still time, Mark. I can hang the picture back up.

To create a dream or vision board, use pictures and words. You can also use motivational words and phrases. Be creative and involve your whole family. Kids love to dream, and they are naturally great at visualizing. Somewhere we adults have lost this skill. Get back in the habit, and make it fun to dream again.

Reminder: Pick which discipline strategy you want to work on first. Write it in your journal and commit to begin implementing it in your life.

Create a Life of Balance

What is it costing you to achieve success? You want to be successful in your work and financial life. There is no need to sacrifice your family or health for business success. Happiness will come when you have balance in all areas of your life.

Your life will not have balance all the time. You want to have a norm that you shift back to whenever you notice things have gotten out of balance. Creating a balanced life is good self-care for you and will set a great example for your family, extended family, friends, and coworkers.

Four Easy Steps to Balance Your Life for Good

Step 1

Create your daily mission or direction. Sit in a quiet place with your journal and list each of the following headings on a separate page.

"What do I want _____?"
Spiritually
Emotionally
Relationally

Intellectually
Financially
Physically

Write down what you want in your life in these six main areas. Some of what you write down will come from previous exercises, or you may include new things that have surfaced since you have started to dream again. {Review what you wrote down in Chapter 4, Start with the End in Mind.}

When you finish, sit back and take a deep breath. How do you feel?

You may want to take a break after this part of the exercise and revisit your list after a few hours or the next day.

Step 2

Next, you will read each list on its own and pick the one item that you want to achieve first in your life. Which one is the most meaningful to you or has the most emotion behind it? That will be the best place to start. Do this for each category.

Write the following question for each in your journal.

What do I want to achieve first? _____,
(spiritually, emotionally, relationally, intellectually,
financially, physically)

You can access the wheel of life tracker at http://margospilde.com/resources

These are the six main areas of focus in your life. How can you create small goals or intentions for each category and maintain balance in your life? These are all things you have decided you want to have in your life. How can you focus on one without eliminating the rest? You can make it happen by creating small intentions, not being discouraged by small setbacks, and allowing grace for yourself not to accomplish everything every day.

Set realistic goals. You have only twenty-four hours in a day, the same as everyone else. You need sleep and nutrition, your family needs your time and attention, and you need to provide quality work for employers or customers. Create time and output goals that allow you to accomplish your objectives with balance in your life. It might work well to use a weekly schedule instead of daily.

Step 3

Write each of your six intentions on one page in your journal. Write them in a present and positive tense.

You may have items that you feel will be impossible to achieve. There may even be items that you will easily achieve in six months or less. The time factor does not matter. Some of the items listed may not feel tangible. It can feel overwhelming to set an intention in an area that has been a struggle to overcome.

You may decide on a thought or belief that needs to shift, but you have been incapable of altering it. You can make the change even if you've never changed previously. Habitual living patterns can be tricky to tweak, and you may not have had everything you needed to make that change before. You have learned much more through this book. All that matters is that it's important to you, and you have a desire to realize it in your life.

Step 4

Intend on doing something every day toward at least one of these intentions. Erase all guilt in your life regarding things not done. You will cover every aspect of your life with these six categories. Your goal is to live a balanced life.

Let's look at a scenario that may throw someone off track. You have a goal of getting in shape and running four days per week. Despite your efforts, there is a huge project at work that requires more time than you anticipated, and it's time for the fall fundraiser at your kid's school. You decide to help set up and take down to support the PTA, and your kids are excited to go to the carnival with you. Of course, you do not exercise this week, and the following week is not looking promising. You did have a great time with your kids, and the committee was grateful for your help.

Instead of feeling bad about your lack of achievement toward your physical health intention, what steps did you make toward your relational goals? You have invested in the relationship with your children and with friends through the school. It feels good to give back, and you have invested your time in a worthy cause that provides emotional benefits to you from donating your time, talents, efforts, and finances. Choose to eliminate any underlying feelings of guilt or regret in lacking achievement toward one goal and celebrate your effort toward other goals.

6

Live Your Life of Excellence

And this is my prayer:
that your love may abound more and more in knowledge
and depth of insight,
so that you may be able to discern what is best
and may be pure and blameless for the day of Christ.
(Philippians 1:9–10 NIV)

LIVING YOUR LIFE of excellence requires determination and perseverance to keep moving forward despite setbacks. You read that in the last chapter. It is so important, I think it bears covering a second time.

- *You will mess up every day, and you may even skip days at a time without a thought of your stated intentions and goals.*
- *Release your guilt and offer yourself grace.*
- *Every step you take forward is good for you.*
- *If you take more steps forward than backward, you are in a better position.*
- *Forget about the things you don't do because that only attracts negative emotions.*

Positivity Draws People toward You

If you have read any books or studies that discuss the vibrational frequencies of our bodies and emotions, you will have heard that positive emotions vibrate at high frequencies. Negative emotions resonate or vibrate at a low frequencies, and in turn, they attract more low-frequency vibrations.

The science of frequency began with Dr. Royal Raymond (Royal Raymond Rife, n.d.), whose career accomplishments began in the late 1920s and ran into the 1930s. Dr. Rife developed a frequency generator that reportedly cured 100 percent in his research study of 1,000 patients with incurable cancer. A series of trouble with physicians changing their support and opinions on his research and a breakin at his lab caused Dr. Rife's research to disappear.

In 1992, Bruce Tainio (Bruce Tainio, n.d.) built the world's first frequency monitor, which studied the human body's frequency and the different frequencies of illnesses and diseases. Tainio's research has led to the effects of frequency on our health, food choices, exercise, mindfulness, and everything that affects the vibrational frequency around us. You may have felt the effects of the vibrational phenomenon and not realized why you felt especially great around a certain individual or the reason you experienced drain or fatigue after a particular encounter.

The first thing to note is "like attracts like," and we tend to stay where we are. We want to stay where it feels comfortable and not different from ourselves. Second, humans are attracted to or pulled toward higher vibrational frequencies, although we often resist going outside our "safe" place. As you move upward and with purpose toward the more heightened vibrational emotions, you will notice that you are attracting more willingness, acceptance, love, joy, and peace. These emotions are what you desire to have more of in your life. It is your life of abundance.

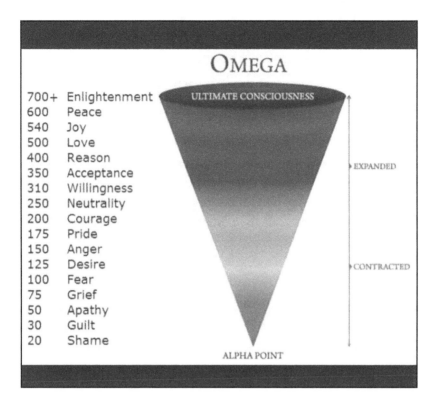

As you can see, enlightenment is at the top of the chart, and guilt and shame are at the bottom. As a young Christian, it was difficult for me to withstand the negativity and hatred of people against God. This graph can explain the belief that light or goodness overtakes darkness more readily. Love in its truest form, which isn't similar to worldly love, comes with complete peace and brings a deep understanding of the peace that passes understanding.

Enlightenment is the source of all that is good. Positivity draws more positivity. People will notice you are different and will enjoy being around you. My hope is for you to experience the highest of highs and spend the rest of your life attempting to get and stay in the place of love, joy, peace, and enlightenment.

Create a Life Plan

You have many demands on your time every day, and your life plan will become your guide for who you want to be in your life. It's important to specify what you value most and how you desire to live and interact in the world. What you want to accomplish in your life will be achieved through action steps, and your life plan will guide you in how to move forward.

Your plan will go together purposely and will not be drastically affected by the hectic nature of life. Most people will not get everything done that they want every single day. If you do, fantastic! Think of how quickly you will see results in that case. However, if you are like me, you will miss the target almost every day, yet you will still see results. Isn't that great to know? Think good thoughts, keep your life plan in front of you, and do the best you can. Excellent daily habits and positive habitual thought patterns are the keys to your success.

Mission

Write the word "MISSION" at the top of a new page in your journal. Look back to your notes in Chapter 5, Create a Life of Balance. Those are your intentions for the six areas of your life.

Next, write down your six intentions under the Mission heading. Ensure that your statements are crafted positively and that they are what you truly want. It often helps when you state them as if they have already been accomplished.

Here is an example from my own life when I was in my thirties:

- *I pray every day.*
- *I provide value to people that they gladly pay me for.*
- *I speak and sound pleasant at all times.*
- *I receive money every day from my intellectual efforts.*
- *I tithe $25,000 a year to my church.*

- *I can see my abdominal muscles through my skin.*

Here is a more recent example from my life in my forties. You can see how it has evolved. Some things were changed, added to, or eliminated. I became a completely different person in those ten years:

- *I provide value to others.*
- *I am worthy of being blessed and highly favored.*
- *I am buying $2.5 million in assets in the coming year.*
- *I buy cash-flowing properties that allow others the opportunity to invest.*
- *I encourage people, build them up, invest in them, and I am a source of wisdom and guidance for others.*

Action

Write your next heading, "ACTION," on a new page. Refer to Chapter 4, Start with the End in Mind, you will list your number one objective. You may want to work this out on a scratch piece of paper first and transfer it to your journal after you have completed the action plan.

Next, look at your list under step 8. Write down all the items you have listed that you must do to achieve your number one objective. You can put them in any order at this point.

Now, go back and prioritize your steps with A, B, C, D, etc. The first or most important step will get an A. Important but not immediate steps get a B, and less important steps will get C, D, and E categories based on their importance. *It will be helpful if you mark very few steps with A because those are immediate needs. If you have ten items listed with an A, you will be in the same place as you are now, overwhelmed and with no direction.*

You will have several categories of steps. Transfer the steps back to your journal. Under your objective, write A and list the A steps with space to make notes and set completion goals.

Continue this format for B, C, D, and E steps in that order. If you think of anything else that needs to be done, write those steps under the proper category. It will help to leave room for additional action steps that may come up. I recently got a one-inch binder and made it my to-do list with tabs for every section of life. It is essentially this process, and because it is a binder, I can add pages as I need them.

Under step A, take note of any actions that you can finish quickly, and take action immediately. Now is always a better time than later. Set a completion goal line and a tentative schedule for completing each task for steps B and beyond.

A goal line is your target date for completion. A goal line can be more positive and motivational than a deadline. Very few people respond well to a deadline. It may feel like a failure if you don't meet that deadline. Instead, give yourself a goal line that will evoke a fun, competitive environment that can keep you going forward, attempting to beat your own goal. If you don't make the goal this time, set a new goal line until you make it. Release your guilt. Do you see a pattern here? Guilt is not your friend. It can be your worst enemy.

The tentative completion date should be sooner than your goal line, which builds a buffer for unexpected delays or life getting in the way. Transfer your dates and tentative schedule to a calendar that you will look at and use. Don't get worked up or stressed out. Instead, focus your excitement on what is ahead.

Intention

Intend on doing something every day toward your mission. You will get there eventually if you continue to move forward. Keep your mission in front of you. When things are out of sight, they will be out of mind. You will get distracted. Distractions come easily, so set a reminder and look at it every day.

We all tend to revert to our old habits. Usually, those unproductive habits have kept us stuck and have brought us to where we are currently. When you consistently put your action steps in front of you, you will be surprised at how effortlessly things start falling into place.

Affirmation

Many people have success with creating affirmations that reflect what they want. It is often helpful to read them aloud. Rather than pressuring yourself to a strict schedule, recognize that you are working toward your end goal every time you read them.

Refer to what you wrote down in previous exercises and get creative with what you want to affirm in your life. It may help to look at what you wrote down for what you do not want and transpose those statements into an opposite statement. Choose what feels most important to your life right now and where you need the most work in your thinking. Rephrase them to be positive and present and combine some of the statements to make more sense. Read them aloud several times to write them accurately to how you speak. See if you can turn your mission into an affirmation.

Make a copy of your affirmations and keep them where you will look at them, with your calendar or journal. Reminding yourself about what you are working toward is an integral part of your Life Plan.

You now have your mission with an action plan, a calendar with goal lines, and affirmations. Set a reminder for yourself to read your affirmations and enjoy the fruits of your labor.

Section II

Taking Action with Your Resources

Preface

SECTION II WILL introduce you to thoughts and ideas on managing money in your household or business. I will introduce concepts that shift your thinking and mindset about money. You will begin to understand the Laws of Increase and Multiplication and how to use your resources differently. Most importantly, you will learn concepts most people have not heard about or learned in school.

It is important to understand your purpose and passion in life, and sometimes when you follow your passion, your financial blessings multiply and expand. It is a blessing to use the special gifts and talents that God has given you to bless people, and in return, to bless your family. That is what we all want.

The most important change you can make is your belief surrounding money. The Bible teaches us concepts about money that still apply today, such as reaping and sowing or the law of increase. Yet the lies about money being bad and making us evil have become socially acceptable to believe. These lies are destructive to everyone and have permeated society today. It does not serve God's kingdom to believe the lie that having money makes you bad.

I intend to educate you on the concepts of abundance to alter negative thinking regarding money. Replace evil, lack, and scarcity with thoughts of goodness, blessing, and abundance. Money is a tool God has given you to grow and advance His kingdom. When you embrace and understand this concept, you will begin to experience abundance and opportunities that you never dreamed were possible.

Everyone's gifts, talents, and purpose will differ and may not include acquiring large amounts of money. However, we all must manage financial resources coming into our households. When you learn and grow in your ability to manage your resources, you will earn greater trust in your knowledge. God will provide increase with the opportunity to manage greater resources. I want you to feel great about the resources that God supplies to you and prepare you to be a great steward of those resources.

7

Live Your Life with Intention

Let them shout for joy and be glad, who favor my righteous cause;
And let them say continually,
"Let the LORD be magnified,
who has pleasure in the prosperity of His servant."
(Psalm 35:27 NKJV)

INTENTIONALLY LIVING YOUR life of abundance is not about money or having more money. It's about your mindset, the strategies you implement, and how you use your resources. You don't need MORE resources; you need to learn to use them differently. Just because things have always been done one way doesn't mean it's the best or the only way. Be intentional about learning new ideas or ways to manage your resources. Seek to understand, be curious, and take action to do things differently. Whatever you choose may take time to implement, and it may not work at all for your situation. The one thing you can count on is this: **If you don't make any changes, you won't get *any* changes.**

Implementing new strategies is not easy, and it's scary most of the time. Making any change in your financial resources can cause much uncertainty and angst. I was slow to implement these strategies for myself. I often hear people say that they wish they had known about something years ago. It doesn't matter what you knew years ago. All that matters is how you move forward. I am extremely thankful for the opportunity to learn these strategies and implement them at my own pace. The information compiled in this section has dramatically changed our family and the hope we have for the future. We are now in control of our financial future. I no longer feel the weight of our financial resources covering less and less as the cost for what we need to live goes up and up.

As stated previously, abundance is not about money or getting rich quickly. Having abundance and prosperity in your life is about living the full, rich life you deserve and enjoying all that God desires for you. You can experience an abundance in every area of your life, including love, joy, peace, happiness, health, passion, focus, purpose, excellence, blessings, friendship, and freedom.

Abundance is not money. Money is only a tool that we use to make our lives easier. You can experience an abundance of money, and you can experience a lack of it. How can you define the role of money in your life? What benefits do you get from having access to money?

What pain do you experience when you don't have enough money? People are often more motivated to avoid pain than to gain pleasure from it. That will keep you in your current state. Your "intention" is a way of moving from your current state into a place _you decide_ you want to be. The first step of intention is to understand your money blueprint, the unconscious rules of money you use in life, and your decision-making.

In Section I, you worked on discovering your purpose in life. Financial resources and money are tools that can help you achieve and grow in that purpose. In Section II, you will work on your willingness to acquire and retain financial resources. Except in severe inability, every adult is responsible for managing resources to live in this world. That is true except where people truly need help and assistance.

Even if your purpose is to be a missionary, you will still need resources to survive and help others. You will always need financial resources to supply yourself and your family with food, clothing, shelter, and basic self-care. No matter your profession, you will need resources to communicate with people, and you will likely have travel or transportation expenses. Although certain occupations such as missionaries may have living expenses and resources supplied from outside themselves, they are still ultimately responsible for acquiring them. Begin now to plan for your future needs and what you will do with your future career transitions.

There are several areas of intention that you can explore relating to your money blueprint, which is your tendency around money and finances. When you are curious about why you think or act in a certain way around money, it will allow awareness into your life. This will enable you to change your thinking and reactions around money. That is how you begin to remove behaviors or habits that do not support your intention.

I once heard Minister Joel Osteen say, "You will never rise any higher than your thinking." That is true in every area of your life, and it is especially true with your finances. Typically, what we learn about money has been learned from people around us, often our family of origin. We do not set out to intentionally "decide" our thoughts about money.

Did your family live paycheck to paycheck? Were the bills something to hate and despise? Was there frequently an unpleasant atmosphere in your home when money came up? Those are all ideas and attitudes around money that you may need to overcome or change. Hopefully, you never stop improving upon your money blueprint, because everyone eventually bumps into a new ceiling or area that can trigger an "I don't deserve this," "I'm not good enough," or "I shouldn't have this" ceiling. Expect more for yourself. Believe you deserve more. God does.

There was a time when I was working on a similar writing project when a new acquaintance inquired about what I was doing. When I told him, his response was, "Oh, prosperity gospel stuff," and he walked away. That phrase was completely foreign to me. Certainly, I had seen the devil's work in turning money into something bad and dirty. It was also readily apparent that it is socially acceptable for Christians to believe and perpetuate the devil's lies about money. Money is the root of all evil, after all. It had never occurred to me that the mindset about how Christians should be poor or not have money would have a title.

Luckily, those lies didn't ring true. After all, there are many stories and lessons in the Bible that have to do with money. Many of Jesus' original followers had come from backgrounds with financial means. God continually used wealthy people to accomplish His work throughout the Bible. Stories abound of a follower's heart turning to God and then attaining much wealth and influence. God wants His followers to be prosperous and succeed, sow good seeds, and be a joyful example of His kingdom. My desire is for you to attain much abundance in the form of freedom, happiness, joy, wealth, and influence on your journey. I want you to prosper and succeed and have more than you asked for or imagined.

Mindset Matters

Every word you put in your head either encourages you to grow or hinders your forward momentum. Find creative ways to let encouraging words enter your head every day. Surround your thoughts with positive and motivating words by listening to uplifting podcasts, books, music, or encouraging speakers. The words you hear will continuously remind you how to speak well to yourself. You can fit this into your busy life by listening to books or podcasts while walking, driving, or working out.

Money and finance is an area where there is much negative self-talk. We don't set out to speak badly to ourselves about money. Mostly, we learn it from the people we spent most of our time with as youngsters. Have you heard the phrase, "More is caught than taught"? That means you learn more from what the adults and influential people around you do than from what they intentionally set out to teach you.

You might recognize the negative self-talk after you hear something like this come out of your mouth: "Money doesn't grow on trees, you know." Where did that phrase come from, and why do we keep passing it down from generation to generation? I have caught myself beginning to say that phrase many times to my children. That's where I used the word "STOP" and thought about what that message says to my children. What is the goal? Is it to stop thinking about how money does not grow on trees? What does that mean about money? Since I didn't want them to be confused about money for their entire lives, I told them what I truly wanted to relay instead.

Since most of what we think about money was "caught" from others, we have probably not changed or challenged those thoughts and internal beliefs. Some Christians will perpetuate the idea that not having money is more spiritual or godly. After all, it is easier for a camel to fit through the eye of a needle than it is for a rich man to go to heaven. I would like to challenge your thoughts about money right now and offer some alternatives that just might change your entire world.

During my tour of the Holy Land, I learned some interesting cultural facts that helped place some of the teachings in the Bible into a much clearer picture. The "eye of a needle" is a smaller, people-sized door inside a giant camel-sized gate door. People could go through the smaller door. When they came in with loaded camels, they would open the big gate that allowed the camel to walk right in without unloading it to get inside. It's a lot of extra work to unpack the camel to make it fit through the smaller door and load it again. Before that insight, the verse about a camel going through the eye of a needle seemed impossible. Now I see it is much more difficult but not entirely impossible. I now understand that a rich man can get into heaven, but the task may be more challenging.

Life is not about money. Abundance is not about money. Money makes paying for housing and buying food for your family a much less time-consuming process. You do, however, need money to survive in the world. Thankfully, we have jobs that pay us for our time since our skills are often not useful in bartering to help pay everyday living expenses.

In most industrialized nations, it would be unpleasant if everyone lived in tents or on the streets. That would make everything unsanitary, and the communities would be full of sickness from the human waste left everywhere. We have many advantages and are motivated to help governments who do not have good, safe water to drink and have not learned the benefits of proper sanitization. Let's appreciate and embrace what money has brought us in gains and improvements.

On a trip to the California coast during the COVID pandemic, my friend and I visited Los Angeles and then rented a hotel room on the beach. I did not choose wisely because the entire boardwalk was a homeless community when we arrived. There were tents, furniture, beds, and many living conveniences piled along the edge of the sand on the boardwalk. It was a happy tent town full of people living directly on the beach on some of the best real estate around.

From our standpoint, we had spent money traveling, renting a car, taking time away from our families, eating at restaurants, and paying for hotel rooms. We did not see the typical beach that we expected coming from Missouri. It was a messy, dirty, unclean, unsightly, and somewhat disgusting homeless camp. We could not enjoy the beach because the giant tent town obstruction was between our hotel and the water.

That experience did not leave us feeling abundant. We had to spend time making reservations at a different hotel, packing the car again, and then driving to a new location. Instead of abundance, I felt my resources were being wasted or squandered. Think about how your actions affect the resources of others. Your choices and actions can increase abundance for others or lessen it. Are you multiplying abundance or multiplying scarcity? When you leave people with a good experience with a smile or a word of encouragement, or when you respectfully express your displeasure, you are helping to multiply abundance for others.

To live in society, we must have resources to establish shelter, food, utilities, and transportation. None of us wants people to be homeless or see others going through life without financial resources. It is unsafe for everyone when people do not have proper living conditions or sanitary conditions. Part of becoming an adult is providing for yourself and your family. You get to decide how you want to live and where. If you need financial resources to live, how can it be bad to acquire resources or desire to enjoy your life?

You get to choose for yourself what you want in your life. Your choices and actions have consequences. Sometimes you might not realize the vast effect your decisions have on others. In the example above, California's rule change was intended to produce goodness. It came from an earnest desire to care for people. Unfortunately, it had many unintended and unpleasant consequences that hurt businesses, property owners, visitors, and more. Be intentional about your choices. Be intentional about what you choose, and be intentional about what you are multiplying in the world.

Habits about Money

The way you think is a habit, and the first step to changing anything, especially bad habits, is becoming aware of what you are doing and why.

1) What are your thoughts and internal dialogue?
2) Why do you do what you do?
3) Where is your biggest opportunity for improvement? Choose which one to work on first.
4) Encourage yourself to find creative ways to think thoughts of abundance.

Read through the list of habits around money and become curious about your habits. You will believe that you have more than enough when you have successfully altered your thought processes regarding lack and scarcity. Miraculously, you will also find that you _do_ have _more than enough_.

Money Mindset Habits

- _Decide that you want your life to be different._

  Deciding is usually the first step, and it's an important one. The series of decisions that come after this will be harder. Make a choice that you want your life to be different. You learned about this in Section I, and now you can confirm your commitment. You get to take action about your decision and make changes about what your life has been and what it will be.

- _Stop thinking about money._

  I have heard people say, "All rich people think about is money." In my experience, it is easy to believe that lie when you do not have large financial means. The truth is that people who have access to plenty of money rarely think about it unless they are managing their money and making decisions around it. Your goal is to understand how differently you think about money when you have plenty of it.

  Excessive thoughts about money come from a place of scarcity or deprivation. How much time do you spend thinking about money?

  - What bills are due and when.
  - What bills you can't pay.
  - When something needs to be fixed.
  - When the paycheck hits the account.

– When choosing to buy the name brand or generic brand.

The list of questions you ask yourself during the day is endless. How much time do you really spend thinking about money? If you are honest with yourself, how much of your thoughts are about not having enough money?

- ***Hope versus hopelessness.***
  My experience has been that when I can't have something I desperately want, it takes on a different role in my life. Have you noticed what happens when rebellious teenagers aren't allowed to do what they want or can't have something that everyone else has? It makes them more motivated to get what they want, and it tends to be all they think about.

  When the feeling of hopelessness accompanies a want or desire, you can become desperate to get it at any cost. That's especially true if you believe you will never get the thing you want and there is no way to change your circumstances. Hopelessness is a self-fulfilling prophesy because it leads to less motivation, which validates your distress.

  Hope changes everything, literally. Think of something you want that you believe you can never have. Now, ask yourself, *What will need to change for me to get it?* What is your answer? Now ask yourself the question again: *What needs to change for me to get that?* Continue asking yourself that question until you get to something that offers you a hint of hope that it might be possible.

  What needs to change for me to get that?
  It's a powerful question.

103

- *Money as a tool or an idol.*

  When you think about money, does it move into an idol position in your life? When my husband got his first "real" job with a "real" paycheck, I found myself spending lots of time managing the money since we had a heavy load of debt to pay off and a new house with no furniture. Through the years of barely getting by, we had postponed making purchases. It was fun to finally be able to buy a new outfit or to eat at a restaurant. Eventually, I found myself spending much time late at night with online banking, and I began to wonder if I had become one of "those" awful rich people who idolize money. Maybe money had become the only thing I wanted. Thankfully, God set me straight. He told me that people who are great with finances will put together a plan to make sure their families are taken care of financially.

  With that new perspective, I quit bashing myself for focusing so heavily on finances. I took care of the finances, ensured everything was paid for, and planned for the future. It is not idolizing money when you set up a financial strategy to accomplish your goals. Once the strategy is in place, you rarely need to think about money. Then your plan will work on a day-to-day basis with shorter check-ins or problem-solving. Once the program is in place, all you have on the agenda is to monitor the results of your plan. At that point, money is simply part of business and life that holds no emotional ties or bondage.

- *Recognize and believe you live in an abundant universe.*

  You live in a world of more than enough. The resources of this planet will not dry up and disappear; we will not use them all up. Humans invent better, more efficient, and alternative options when using too many resources. Human ingenuity will figure out what to do if there isn't enough to sustain our current population growth. People have always evolved to get better and more efficient. There is no reason or proof to believe that the future will be different.

Humans will continue using resources in new and more efficient ways. We might find better ways to acquire, transport, and store resources. Think back to how people lived 150 years ago. There was no electricity, cars, airplanes, or indoor plumbing. We have abundant resources and intellectual power to create. There are so many abundant resources available to us that we may not even imagine how or where to use them in the future.

It is often a big joke when an older generation talks about what they didn't have growing up. Why does every generation say the same thing? Isn't that curious? Instead of feeling sad and nostalgic, stand in awe of how your life has changed for the better. Be thankful and embrace the changes. Do you remember life before computers? How have advances in technology made your life better? What can you easily do now that was more difficult and time-consuming previously?

- *Know that money is not evil.*

  Having money does not make you a bad person. If you believe that money is evil and all rich people are evil, will you want money to enter your life? Probably not, because that would make you evil. If that is your underlying belief system, you will subconsciously move away from having money to avoid being categorized as "evil." That would work against your intention of supplying yourself and your family with the financial resources they need to live and survive on the planet. Intention and changing your thinking patterns are keys to your success.

- *Remove fear from your life.*

> *The only thing we have to fear is fear itself.*
> *(Franklin D. Roosevelt,*
> *Inaugural Address, March 4, 1933)*

I have known this quote for many years; however, I did not realize that I did not understand it until recently. It means there is no fear in the world except the fear that you or another person creates in your mind. When you feel fear and anxiety take hold, ask yourself this question: "What is the worst that can happen?" Answer the question for yourself and choose to react differently in the situation.

What if it looked as if your company were getting bought out and you were afraid of losing your job? Instead of letting fear grip you and take your imagination to all kinds of terrible places, say, "STOP," and ask yourself this question:

What is the worst that *can happen?*

Call to Action

What is the worst that can happen?

Ask yourself this question until you have exhausted all of the worst-case scenarios. You will find the worst isn't as bad as you thought it would be.

Is it that you could not pay your mortgage and might lose your house?

Ask it again, *what is the worst that can happen?*

We might have to move in with my parents until we can figure it out.

What is the worst that can happen?

We might have to live with my parents for a long time if I can't find another job.

My credit might be bad for a while, and it will be crowded with my parents.

What is the worst that can happen?

It would be terrible living with my parents. I would hate it.

Continuing to ask yourself to discover the worst is an excellent practice that gives you more awareness and less fear. You are learning to stop the fear cycle in your thoughts sooner to create new, more useful habits.

None of the scenarios are ideal. The situation won't kill you, and you will get through it. Fear will have less control over you when you gain perspective and let go of the fear.

- *Create value.*

    Money is a result of the value you are creating for the marketplace. The most important thing you can do for yourself and your family is figuring out where you bring the most value. What value are you creating? What are you providing that improves and enhances the world and the people around you?

An easy place to start is by creating something you can do on the side. Take a hobby you love and turn it into something that creates value for others. Work toward a new career or train in areas that give you access to promotions. You are in control of your life. Figure out how to make it happen.

I have found that the best way to get ahead is to take massive amounts of action in a short period. Humans can endure anything when it is temporary. That is another reason why freedom is so valuable. It is tolerable to know that you need to do this for only a short time.

Farming requires a huge amount of action in a short time. The planting season is hectic, stressful, and time-consuming. All the seeds need to go into the ground at the same time when the weather is perfect. Harvest is just as hectic when everything ripens at the same time and needs harvesting before it goes bad.

Expect some chaos once you have found the area where you create the most value through your passion and purpose. Be willing to invest time when it's needed, and anticipate that bursts of activity will be required. You are soon on your way to living your life of abundance.

- *Enjoy your life.*

Have fun with your family, your kids, your spouse, and with your friends. Create a sub-account for entertainment so you can enjoy your life without guilt. Often, one spouse has more difficulty or is more controlling with money. The other spouse may stress less about spending or may not be good at saving it.

Every concert suggestion or night out was an agonizing decision for me at one time. I wanted to buy the cheapest tickets or wait to decide. We would end up playing minigolf at the $7 course or renting a movie. Now, I automatically put money in the entertainment account every month. As the very controlling money spouse, I can say that the travel and entertainment account has freed me to enjoy myself immensely.

Recently, we found out that Nelly would be close to us in concert. Spontaneously, I bought tickets in the closest seats to the stage for the kids and me to go to the show. I didn't even fret for a moment. If we're going to see Nelly, we should be close and enjoy the experience. That is joy, abundance, and happiness.

- *Mitigate the risk of loss to credit, assets, or shelter.*
  Make protecting the security of yourself and your family a top priority. There are many ways to mitigate risk in your household. Here are a few suggestions:

  1) Lower overall debt or mandatory payments.
  2) Improve cash flow.
  3) Have multiple sources of income.
  4) Increase savings.
  5) Create a side gig that brings in additional income.
  6) Retain ample reserves.
  7) Purchase assets that produce passive income outside of your job.
  8) Decrease spending for a short time to increase cash.

Income protection is another descriptor for life insurance. It helps you protect income earners with life insurance, disability insurance if needed, and various other sources. There is a reason that your mortgage and car loan requires you have proof of insurance for your personal property. Why not put the same effort into protecting the primary source of income until you reach a state of financial independence.

Attitudes about Money

It can be difficult to believe that abundance surrounds you when all you experience is lack. There are many paths, journeys, and options for accomplishing the goal of spending less than you earn. You get to decide what works best for you. Do you want to live on less, or do you want to make more? Where can you cut? Do you consider short-term cuts or long-term lifestyle changes? What are your gifts and strengths? What is the best strategy to get from where you are now to where you want to be?

You can only manage money. You cannot control it. Things are going to be out of your hands. Stuff will go wrong, emergencies will happen, brakes will wear out, and trees will fall over spontaneously on the neighbor's fence. Plan for emergencies, knowing that they WILL happen.

Give up control. Give your best effort, manage your finances diligently, and have fun periodically. The rest of it is out of your control. Relinquishing control might be the hardest thing to do, and if you are a control freak, it is almost impossible. Live below your means and plan for nothing to go as planned. You should feel good knowing we're all in the same position. Be flexible. You can decide what you want to happen and develop options for achieving it. Try one thing to see if it works and try something else to see if that works better.

Fear intensifies the challenges you are facing. Fear can destroy your results and ruin your finances. Negative consequences are compounded by fear or freaking out. In moments of high stress and anxiety, calm your mind and practice some deep-breathing exercises. They will help you put effort toward remaining calm and thinking rationally.

People tend to make more impulsive decisions in high-stress moments. ***Fear exacerbates*** problems, and people often make hasty decisions when facing a crisis. Give yourself permission to take the time you need before getting too far into a bad decision-making moment.

You achieve a greater capacity for more in your life when you understand your *money temperament.*

Your *money temperament* explains your tendency toward money such as your habits, attitude, emotions, and values around money. Everyone has the tendency to respond emotionally around money; logical and rational are not the norm. Do you tend to be a saver or spender? Experts suggest the two categories of saving or spending require further depth to differentiate the varieties in our money tendencies. There can be anywhere from five to eight category subsets that further narrow down your money persona.

Not having money saved for large expenses or an emergency was a huge challenge for me. Things would feel out of control when I didn't know where the money would come from to pay for an obligation we owed. Notice your temperament around money and how you react in various scenarios. How do you sound, speak, react, or proceed during various financial conversations? When I am speaking sharply and sounding irritated about the finances, it becomes time to get curious and ask myself, "I wonder what is going on with me?"

Change Your Thinking to Change Your Life

So far, you have learned new ways of thinking about yourself. You have also discovered several ideas and discipline strategies that you can use to change your thinking. These will aid you in reaching your passion and in finding freedom in your life. The title of this book is *Live Your Life of Abundance.* How do you shift your mindset from mediocre living to abundant living? At this point, you will begin to implement small changes and new habits in your life. It will take new ways of thinking, as I have introduced in previous chapters. You are now beginning the change process.

All change begins small and can become the catalyst for big results in your habits, actions, and motivations. The following ideas can change your thinking to yield big results in your financial life. You may want to implement them slowly and stack more concepts onto those you have already implemented. These ideas will alter your current reality and teach your brain new patterns, actions, and behavior.

- *Have cash.* Always keep cash in your purse, wallet, pocket, or all of these. Physically have money available to you at all times. It doesn't matter if you use your debit card. This way you will see money is available all the time.

Mindset = I always have plenty of money.

- *Leave money in your house*, your fire safe, and your secret hiding places. Have jars of change, keep cash in your drawers, and have money in an envelope available whenever you need it.

Mindset = Money is readily and easily available.

The more that money is readily and easily available, the more you will believe you have plenty of money. Years ago, we got cash before going on vacation. Times had changed, and I used only our credit card during the trip. When we got home, I had several $100 bills left over and decided to stash them in a fake decorative book in our living room rather than driving them back to the bank.

My thought process was that the safe is an obvious place to look if you are a thief looking for something to steal. I also do not keep jewelry worth any value in my jewelry box because that is way too obvious. Years later, my husband remembered the cash I had put in the book. I, of course, had moved it so the money wouldn't get stolen. Thankfully, I found the fake book safely hidden in our house. At that point, it was a legitimate threat that I would donate a fake cardboard book to charity and never remember I had stashed money inside.

Mindset = Everywhere I look, I find money.

- *Pay yourself first.* You owe it to yourself and your family to first take care of your finances. Set up transfers that automatically go to savings on payday. Subtract the money for vacation, savings, or credit card bills immediately from your balance. You automatically set up a system to reward yourself with freedom when you live below your means.

Mindset = I live on less than I earn.

Transfer money to your emergency fund first, and then start your entertainment account. When your emergency fund is satisfactory, begin saving for other areas such as a surplus account, college, retirement, a big vacation, or purchasing a rental property.

- *Reward yourself* for your hard work by putting money into your entertainment account.

Mindset = We enjoy life and do fun things.

It was difficult for me to take money out of the budget when there was so little to pay the bills or buy groceries. When you work toward freedom and abundance, all of your family members will experience more hope after having a reward for their dedication, and you can all continue to work together as a team.

- *Create multiple streams of income.* Some people call these "side gigs." Anything you can do that adds increased income for your family can fund your freedom and life of abundance. Your motivation will increase when you are working toward a specific target.

**Mindset = When I am faithful with a little,
I will be entrusted with a lot.**

A secondary reward will occur as you increase income through multiple income streams. You can reduce your taxable income by having a legitimate business. Eventually, you will find that momentum starts to take over, and your financial goals and dreams don't feel as overwhelming.

- *Begin a security account.* You will feel more abundant when you have a surplus, reserves, emergency fund, or security account. Most of us long for greater security. You will avoid potential risk when you have an account with a balance in it. Emergency funds sound boring and a little negative, whereas the title Security Account gives you what you desire and sounds more abundant.

Mindset = We can manage anything that comes our way.

It doesn't matter which account you start with first as long as you start. It also doesn't matter what names you use. Pick what works best for you. Decide if you prefer one large account or multiple smaller accounts.

- *Be diligent and provide for your family.* Believe in something new for yourself. Being faithful and diligent is admirable. When you always have at least one account with a balance, you will always have money readily available.

Mindset = Money is always readily available.

- *Get competitive.* Make a game out of your accounts getting bigger. Do you prefer that they get bigger rather than shrink or disappear? Think of your accounts as similar to pouring sand into a pile. Much of the sand will fall away. It never seems to get as big as the amount of sand you are pouring on top, yet eventually, you will notice the pile gets quite large after much effort in pouring. Here's another mindset shift.

Mindset = No matter what happens in life, our pile keeps growing bigger.

Being financially solvent is extremely important in business. Shouldn't it be just as important to your family's finances? If a company does not maintain a certain amount of cash reserves, it will look bad financially and will become a bad investment. Banks won't loan them money, stock prices may drop, and they could have difficulty negotiating contracts. Future growth will suffer if they don't remain diligent in their finances. If having cash is so important to businesses, why do average Americans not recognize the importance and value of having money available while running their household?

- *Quit being surprised.* Knowing what comes in and what goes out of your financial household is part of being a responsible adult. Ignoring or avoiding the truth will only set you up for failure. Face the truth of your current reality, own it, and take action.

Mindset = I am the master of my finances.

Be diligent with your finances, even if things currently look rough. What is important is that you have a true picture of reality. If there isn't enough money to pay all the expenses, be truthful. If you spend everything on impulse buying or frequent binge shopping, come clean and quit acting surprised.

- *Spend less money during the **year** than you earn.* The bigger the gap between what you earn this year and what you spend determines how much financial freedom you have in your life. The difference also determines how much you believe in abundance for your situation. Don't get hung up on the day-to-day spending when you can achieve success for the year.

Mindset = My income will be much higher than my expenses this year.

You could become a minimalist to create financial freedom. The reality is that a minimalist is more likely to create financial freedom than most and will achieve it sooner. <u>It's not about how much you make. It's about choices and how you manage the money that comes into your household</u>. In essence, your results depend more on what you keep and which strategies you use.

- *Stretch yourself beyond your financial capacity.* Everyone has a money limit or financial boundary that will cap how much you believe you can earn. That amount will be your financial capacity. The limit will also set the upper threshold for how much money you can have in your possession for reserves or savings.

Mindset = My capacity grows bigger and bigger every day.

I have listened to people who have reached their upper limit of money in their life. They will begin to explain what they need to do with the money or decide where to spend it.

You can hear people talk about all the possible scenarios and ways to put that money to good use.

One of my friends has a lucrative business and has successfully made money in real estate. After an extremely successful year, I kept hearing him mention how much he needed to find a place to put some money. I asked him this question: "Why do you need to do something with that money?" He said he had already funded his emergency reserves, and he needed to do something with the extra.

I asked how he knew he had plenty of reserves and why this money couldn't be additional reserves. He responded that he had saved plenty of money and didn't need many months of reserves. After several similar conversations, I was beginning to get suspicious that he had reached his saving limit threshold. Then he added, "It's just sitting in the bank doing nothing. I have to find somewhere to put it."

We discussed how he appeared to be uncomfortable with the amount of cash he had saved. Although he had worked hard to earn that money and lived on less than he earned, he still had an unconscious need to "do something with that money" so he could get back to where he felt more comfortable. We all continuously reach our ceiling or threshold and need to work through those limitations so our capacity can grow bigger.

Call to Action

List all the benefits that you will get from having $10,000 in a security/reserves/surplus account.

Don't decide where you will spend it. You are not spending any of the money. What are your benefits from having it?

8

Life Your Life of Lessons

*The Lord bless you and keep you; the Lord make his face
shine on you and be gracious to you;
The Lord turn his face toward you and give you his peace.
(Numbers 6:24–26, NIV)*

HAVE YOU NOTICED how the same problems keep coming back into your life? Do new problems seem similar to previous ones? It could be a sign that there is a pattern you keep repeating and a lesson you need to learn. What is the negative pattern or challenge teaching you? What do you need to learn from it?

Take note of what you notice and what you might need to learn. I saw a pattern because I would not react well whenever we had an unexpected or large expense. I would lash out at my spouse and children and be very cranky and irritable until I had time to adjust to the large financial outlay. Even though I could plan for unexpected expenses, it seemed my response did not improve with planning.

Transformational change happens when you experience a different, new, and better result from your changed behavior that elicits a response from others that's different than what you expect to happen. It comes from others seeing facial expressions or body language that doesn't express shame or disappointment, or that causes someone to get away from you for thinking or feeling what you shared. The new feelings and improved responses are different from what you expected and are used to getting from the people in your life. When you experience a difference, it will motivate you to continue creating more transformational experiences in your life. You may even become passionate about seeing others share in transformation growth as well.

That process correlates to lessons you need to learn to increase your capacity for abundance and growth and translates to the money lessons discussed in this chapter.

Learning Your Lessons

When we were on a road trip from Denver to Montana, we spent the night in Jackson Hole, Wyoming. The next morning, running behind schedule as was my typical pattern, our car quit working in the middle of an extremely busy intersection. People were honking and yelling at us. We were only one block from the hotel where we had spent the night. I was beginning to think we should have stayed in bed.

Eventually, some nice people helped us push the car out of the intersection, and a tow truck came to drive us to the Ford dealership on the edge of town. It was interesting to view the town from up there on the tow truck with my windows rolled down. People were waving and smiling at us as if we were in a parade, probably because they were no longer trapped behind us at the intersection. I had lots of time to think from that high perspective.

The closer we got to the dealership, the more stressed out I became. How much is this going to cost? Is this car with over 150,000 miles a total loss? What kind of issue and expense will require fixing? Should we buy another car and keep going? Should I rent a car so I'm not late for my next destination? Will I have to come back to Jackson Hole, which is not on the way? Every potential plan and question would cost so much time and money.

It was an all-day deal getting to the Ford dealership on one side of the tourist town. We then had to find an Uber to the airport on the other side of town to get a rental car. Finally, we were loaded and ready to leave Jackson Hole. It was now extremely late in the day with three kids, a dog, the cooler, and massive amounts of luggage loaded into the rental van. Nobody had eaten since the hotel breakfast, and we stopped a few miles from the airport for dinner on our way out of town.

As the waitress took our food order, my phone rang. The repairs were finished. "What!?! You must be kidding me!" I could not have gotten my car repaired that quickly at home with a scheduled appointment. All that was wrong with the car was a tear in the air filter. First off, that repair does not seem important enough for an entire day of pain and agony. It ended up costing very little to fix, and it had taken all afternoon to get to this restaurant three miles out of town.

I wondered how I would get back to the car dealership before it closed and then return the rental car to explain the situation to them with one driver. If I made it this far, the rest should be easy. Everything worked out, and we finally left for Montana before dark. For the first time in my life, I had not freaked out or lost my cool with our impending financial doom. It cost almost as much to Uber across Jackson Hole twice as it did to fix the minor mechanical problem. I was pleasant, adaptive, and willing to spend whatever was necessary to resolve the issue. That attitude was highly out of the ordinary for me.

It's interesting to note that I do not recall any major financial setbacks since that incident in Jackson Hole. Maybe I have finally learned my lesson on how to handle emergencies and sudden high expenditures. My money lesson was to remain calm, recognize that I have prepared for emergencies, and remember that things are typically not as bad as they seem. Learning your money lessons will bring you more abundance, less strife, and most certainly greater joy and happiness.

Money Lessons

Forget Results

The results are out of your hands, so stop pressuring yourself to get results. When you do what you are supposed to be doing, the results will take care of themselves. Think about the possibility that when something doesn't work out as you hoped, it may be for a reason. Maybe that experience opens you up to receive something better in your life. What if there is something bigger and better? The crossroads you are in, the difficult season you have right now, might be preparing you to have the capacity for the blessings and abundance that are coming next in your life.

The only things you can control are your actions and your attitude. When you take action and move toward your dreams, passion, and purpose, the forward momentum and inertia will be in your favor. Do your best, and keep moving. There is no reason to experience any pressure because your action and momentum will propel you forward.

Ask yourself often, or at the end of every day, "Have I done my best?" If you have done your best for that day, you have done all that is required of you. It helps to ask yourself the right questions that give you useful results: "Did I do what I was supposed to do?" "What could I have done differently today or in this situation?" "How can I behave differently in the way I show up next time?" When you answer those questions and view your situation and actions with curiosity, you have done all that you can do.

Be aware of what actions you are choosing. If you sit around the house watching TV, staring at video games, scrolling through social media, or playing golf every day, don't expect to get something in return. You might be disappointed in the results if there aren't any.

For even when we were with you, we used to give you this order:
if anyone is not willing to work, then he is not to eat, either.
(2 Thessalonians 3:10 ESV)

Start somewhere, start anywhere. Your action will lead you where you need to be, and the results are not up to you.

Your Past Does Not Equal Your Future

Past results do not determine your future results. You have the power to change your circumstances, your situation, and your life. There is one sure way of remaining where you are in life: to believe things will always be the same and you can't do anything about it. If you continue to believe you will always get the results you have always gotten, you will. When you speak to yourself and the people around you that there is no hope of anything different, you are right. Henry Ford has a famous quote. I have been on both sides of this quote, and both times, I was right. Try it out for yourself and see what changes in your life:

Whether you believe you can or not, you're right.

Sometimes we can fool ourselves into believing that something else or someone else is stopping us from moving forward. Our brains are fast and adept at deception and reasoning. Be alert when you hear the word "but" as part of your explanation. Maybe you aren't using that word specifically, ***but*** it's silently in your mind. Take note of that as well.

At Wednesday night church, a small group gathered to pray for people who desired healing. An older woman sitting near me began to share her husband's medical challenges. She continued to talk about their situation, and although she never used the word "but," it was certainly understood as you can see in our conversation:

"I want my husband to be healed. We can't get in to the doctor. We need to see the doctor."

I said, "God can heal without a doctor."

She said, *but* "God heals through doctors"; *but* "We can't get an appointment to see one"; *but* "We have been praying for hours and days"; *but* "We need an appointment"; *but* "They haven't called to give us an appointment"; *but, but, but.*

It went on and on with statements like these.

Later I said, "After all of us praying for your husband, can you do something for him tonight?"

She said, *but* "I've already done that. We've been praying all day, and it hasn't worked"; *but* "He needs a doctor, and he can't be healed without a doctor."

Unfortunately, she continued to tell me how important it was for him to get a doctor's appointment and why she had already done everything to heal him. And nothing had happened yet.

I was a bit frustrated and sad that she was limiting God's ability to heal her husband. She needed it to be done the way she believed it should be done. Although God can heal through doctors, it doesn't mean He has to heal through doctors. This woman was limiting God, which minimized the opportunities for healing her husband. It's the same when we place limits on ourselves. The world is full of abundance and opportunities to get what you want in life. Don't limit yourself and minimize your options to get what you want.

Shake Off Complacency

It's important to understand that things don't show up in your life without effort and intention working toward them. If you are a parent, you might understand how much you desire to give and do for your children. As our kids get older, they have the capacity and skills to do things for themselves. I feel very proud when they express their desires and show me how they are willing to get what they want in life. It is much different from when they could not decide on their own or take steps to achieve what they wanted. I deeply desire for my children to decide what they want in life, to work toward their goals, and to include me in their quest to achieve them.

Your heavenly Father feels the same about you. The more you work toward your goals and dreams, the more He wants to give you. I desire to help my children's efforts go further and accomplish more. It's a blessing for us to have the education, skills, and resources to help them achieve more than they ever thought or imagined. When we help our children see success, they will take it and extend that success further than you could ask or imagine. You get the same effort and help toward your actions. It is a multiplication of your efforts and intention. The result will undoubtedly be more than you thought was possible.

Have you experienced the age range of eleven to thirteen when children begin to feel entitled to have anything and everything they want? It seems the age when marketing begins to take hold of their undeveloped brains. I have gotten frustrated with the list of demands coming from children who didn't do what I asked and needed prodding to accomplish the smallest tasks.

Adults sometimes have similar expectations. We want the fancy car, to live in the big house, and to go on a dream vacation while not putting forth the work required to reach those goals. Choose diligence over complacency and expect different results.

It is typical for me to get discouraged. Now I bounce back more quickly, which allows a momentary lull in my attitude to not affect my results.

God rewards those who are intentional and diligent. There are two verses I like to keep in mind when I don't "feel" like doing anything:

Lazy hands make a man poor, but diligent hands bring wealth.
(Proverbs 10:4 NIV)

The soul of a lazy man desires, and has nothing;
but the soul of the diligent shall be made rich.
(Proverbs 13:4 NKJV)

Quit Comparing

Comparison to others and jealousy multiply the wrong thing for yourself. When you are genuinely happy that others have received great things in their lives, it multiplies your joy and happiness and theirs. You probably want more joy and happiness in your life rather than jealousy, hatred, or scarcity.

When you are jealous about someone else's success, notice how bad it feels for you. Do you get angry, irritated, or mad at yourself? Have you heard yourself exclaim, "They didn't deserve that!"? Or did you attribute the blessing they received to something that had nothing to do with their efforts? Do you believe they got it with none of their effort or decide, "It's just not fair"?

That is not abundance thinking, and you probably would not like it if you heard someone saying that about you. Multiplication and abundance give you more of what you are giving away. Be intentional about what you are giving away, and notice what you multiply around you. We have all learned patterns of thinking that are not helpful or abundant. It is possible to change those patterns and be intentional about what you multiply and put out in the world.

Even if the other person doesn't know or hear what you think, it affects your brain. It comes out in your behavior. You may not say it out loud or mumble under your breath. Your kids are like video recorders with legs. They will see and listen to your behavior and take that belief with them for the rest of their lives. Decide to be intentional about not comparing yourself and your life to others. Not comparing yourself to others will help you eliminate jealousy and unpleasant feelings when viewing social media as well.

Purpose of Money

Before industrialization, resources came from specialized skills, the ability to labor, and one's place in the surrounding community. Society is more efficient now as employees and large businesses produce larger quantities versus small batches. We live in a global economy instead of a local community, and money takes the place of barter. Money allows us to be more productive and to acquire resources to live more easily. Money is not evil; it is necessary to live. The purpose and use of money is a tool, not something to be ashamed of or avoid.

The purpose of money is to provide for you and your family's needs. It supports the government, provides for churches, and helps others who cannot provide for themselves. The biggest impact of money is to multiply resources that will meet additional needs.

If you have grown a garden or lived on a farm, you will understand how agriculture produces in abundance. The system of sowing and reaping produces multiples of anything planted. Farming, planting seeds, and the process of reproduction are pure forms of abundance. One turns into many. One animal can produce offspring numerous times throughout its reproductive lifecycle. Everything that grows will reproduce more of what is planted to flourish, not die out, or cease to exist in the world.

According to Liz Lemon on *30 Rock*, the purpose of money is simple: "I want to do that thing rich people do where they turn money into more money."

This skit might make us laugh, but the simplicity of it is wonderful when we compare what Liz Lemon said to the story of the talents in Matthew 25:14–30. Notice how the purpose is to use money, multiply it, and turn it into more money. This parable is worth reading.

A devotion in the YouVersion Bible app titled "3 Financial Lessons from the Parable of the Talents" considers three lessons that you can learn from the parable. The first lesson is that stewards must take risks and take action. You learned how important it is to mitigate risk in a previous chapter. Equally important is taking action.

The second lesson in the study considers is how not to compare yourself to others. It says we are all given gifts according to our abilities. The three people in the parable did not receive the same number of talents initially or at the end. Each person was blessed according to his abilities and gifts.

The third and most important lesson from the study is that our money and resources on this earth are not our own. We cannot take it with us when we are done on the earth, and we are called to be good stewards of the resources that we have been entrusted with during our time on earth. You can read this story yourself in Matthew 25 and decide how it compares to your belief system. If you are feeling a change in your heart toward the role of money in your life and the way God views finances, journal that experience for yourself and be open to seeing what changes take place in your finances.

As Christians, our responsibility is to love one another and to multiply the resources entrusted to us for the betterment of God's people. Money is not bad or evil; it is a gift and blessing from God. You are obligated to faithfully flourish and thrive on this planet by planting seeds and multiplying everything that is entrusted to you.

Time is our most precious resource, and we easily waste it and give it away for little value. The challenge with trading time for money is the inherent scarcity of your own time. You cannot create more time for yourself, and you can never recover the hours that you have lost. The only way to multiply it is to leverage the time of others who are willing to help work toward another person's dream in return for a guaranteed paycheck.

There are many great reasons to trade your time for money, and most people will become employees in society today. We need help with insurance, taxes, retirement accounts, education, trades, and skills. The list of things that we cannot do for ourselves goes on and on. We live in a heavily regulated and complex world. Employers who are willing to navigate these confusing areas are a huge blessing. Being employed, however, doesn't mean you must eliminate the purpose of money from your life or choose to live paycheck to paycheck for the rest of your days. You have choices and options. You can choose to put yourself and your family first and work smarter, not harder.

9

Live Your Life of Freedom

For you were called to freedom.
Only do not use your freedom as an opportunity for the flesh,
but through love, serve one another.
(Galatians 5:13, ESV)

FREEDOM IS ABOUT accquiring the resources you need to live the life you want. Simply put, financial freedom is having more financial resources coming into your household than what you need to pay for your fixed and variable costs of living. There are several ways of accomplishing financial freedom, and you get to decide what combination you will use to achieve your goal of financial independence and freedom. A common misconception is that financial independence is about the constant drive for increasing income and incurring a lavish lifestyle. Some people may desire more, more, more, but those people will likely never be satisfied or achieve freedom.

You get to "decide what you want." How do you want to live? What do you want for your family? You get to choose, you have autonomy, and you have choices. The definition of "autonomy" is **freedom from external control, influence, or independence.** Income freedom, financial independence, or financial freedom is not something that many of us learned to aspire to or accomplish for ourselves. In rich or poor households, children are rarely taught anything beyond working for someone else and spending what they earn on anything they want at the moment.

Growing up, we observed people working for money, paying bills, running out of money, and continuing to toil at their jobs. No one taught us to understand purpose or passion and why our parents were working besides earning a paycheck. Freedom was not a topic that anyone brought up during the first twenty-five years of my life. Did anyone bring this up during your formative years? Although nobody brought it up to me, financial freedom is what I wanted for myself. It was deep inside of me. I just didn't know that it had a name or that it was possible.

The United States was founded on the principles of freedom. Freedom is what motivated people to immigrate to the great country of the United States. It is why people still want to immigrate to the United States and pursue the American Dream. Sometimes it is difficult to know what we want until we no longer have it, and that is when we become motivated to get what we don't have. Most of us have grown up with choices, and we haven't experienced the pain that goes along with not getting to choose for ourselves. Think about all the wars and conflicts that have allowed people the continued freedom of choice.

Freedom is autonomy.

Autonomy is making your own choices and decisions.

Making your own choices and decisions is the opportunity to DECIDE what you want for your life.

Opportunity to decide your own life and fate is good for everyone.

A recent example of fighting for the freedom to choose is the conflict over requiring the COVID vaccine. Most of us have been vaccinated for other conditions during our lifetimes. Vaccines are required for schools and elsewhere. Our opportunity to choose was taken away from us years before we could decide. Now that we get to decide for ourselves, many people choose to refuse it. We don't like to give up our ***right to choose for ourselves.*** That is truly the issue driving this debate. People crave the freedom to make their own decisions and resist when others decide for them.

Polio is present in only two countries in the world. Very few parents fear their children will be paralyzed from polio. The polio vaccine has been in place for over five decades. There was no threat to our decision-making or autonomy. We simply got the vaccine, moved on with our lives, and did not think anything about it. We were no longer faced with the choice to be vaccinated or not until COVID. When a nurse brought in multiple syringes to inoculate our kids, it was natural and common. The discussion took place about vaccines years ago, and we didn't need to spend energy deciding for ourselves.

The process of not needing to make a decision often keeps us stuck in the same financial scenario that our parents and grandparents lived. When we don't need to choose how to live our lives, we simply do what we have always done. It is often easier not to make a choice. The way we manage our finances was decided decades ago. It frees us up not to spend time or energy making those decisions. We do what everyone has modeled for us and taught us previously. Guess what—you get to decide for yourself, and you don't need to do what everyone else has done before you.

Bonnie Ware, a palliative nurse from Australia, wrote a book called *The Top Five Regrets of the Dying*. Bonnie talked with people at the end of their lives, which is when they tend to be most reflective. After talking with them, she wrote of the common themes that came up repeatedly when she asked her patients about their greatest regrets in life. Here are the top two regrets. It is interesting to note they both have a deep connection to what you have been reading:

1. I wish I'd had the courage to live a life true to myself rather than what others expected of me.
2. I wish I hadn't worked so hard.

Another regret is this: "I wish I had let myself be happier." Three of the five top regrets are directly connected to the information you are learning to implement. People often want freedom and don't realize it is available or possible for them. It is possible to live with autonomy and freedom. It is possible to achieve financial security, income independence, financial freedom, and control in your life. You have the opportunity to choose.

A misconception that persists is that freedom or independence means that you don't or won't work ever again. Freedom is about choices and limiting the control from outside sources. Freedom and autonomy eliminate the belief that you "have" to do something when it isn't the best choice for you. Living passively while others supply your every need is not living your life. Studies show that when people "retire" and sit at home without passion or purpose, their life is dramatically less happy. They also get sick more often and don't live as long.

When you have autonomy and freedom, you will likely find that you want to use your brain, creativity, and gifts to provide value to the world. The people who live the longest with the most joy are not sitting at home on their couches. They are following the passions in their hearts and recognizing how their gifts and talents offer greatness to the world. You get to choose the job, career, business, side gig, part-time opportunity, service, or volunteer opportunity that best suits your needs and gives you the most happiness. You get to decide what is right for you. Make it happen in your life. You will feel awesome when you are working toward what you want. Suddenly, you may notice that some of your circumstances are no longer burdening you. You have outgrown them.

Like most of you, my story did not start with a desire to have a lot of money or live a lavish lifestyle. What I wanted was the freedom to do what I wanted. I did not want to ask someone when or if I could go somewhere. I especially resisted the two-week vacation rule. During my first year working after college, I had to save one hundred percent of my vacation time for our wedding and to go on our honeymoon. It was necessary for me to neglect self-care for an entire year to meet this future need. What I wanted was to have both/and.

It can take a relatively small budget for me to enjoy life. I prefer to live with few debts and bills. My basic needs are to fund my business, personal growth habits, and most importantly, travel expenses. The great news is that YOU get to decide what YOU require for your life. Figure out your basic needs, what you prefer, and what you can do to create a match between your income and your expenses.

You also get to decide what is important for you outside of your basic needs and dreams. What do you like or prefer? What is important for you that gives you joy? I prefer to splurge on comfortable and stylish shoes and luxury handbags. It is easy to quickly judge people by what you see on the outside or perceive their lives as similar to what you see on TV or movies. My truth is that I buy my expensive items used or at a deep discount. Full retail price is not what I prefer, and I don't want to pay what marketing tells me something is worth. You get to decide what is important for you.

We always buy used cars, RVs, boats, motorcycles, and golf carts, and we typically own them long after they are paid off. I prefer to buy after others have taken the worst depreciation while purchasing new. It is important that we take care of what we own so we can enjoy it for years to come. I also don't switch houses because it costs too much to buy, sell, and move to another home. We are currently over ten years into a thirty-year mortgage, and I am resisting the possibility of downsizing since inflation gives us the option to buy much less than we have now. What is important to you?

Figure out your non-negotiables. When you decide that you are serious about creating freedom in your life, take these three steps to dig deeper into the ideas and concepts you read in this book. Next, take action on one of the ideas. Be intentional about what you will do next that will change the direction of your life and make things better for the long term.

1. Research: Read through the ideas and concepts in this chapter and dig into them further. Do your research.
2. Pick One: Choose only one of the ideas to implement in your personal situation and make it happen for yourself.
3. Take Action: Do something toward implementing one thing you choose to implement first.
4. Document: Write down the steps you will take next. Put them on your calendar and to-do list.

Once you master the first idea or concept and begin to see the benefits from implementing just one of these ideas, you will be motivated to learn and implement more of them. Your research and implementation will yield a new understanding, and it will prepare you to discover additional concepts that you read in this chapter.

Expectations of Money

Money Is a Tool

Money is a tool we need to live in this society. Living an abundant, happy, and joyful life requires financial resources. That is the bottom line. You must have access to money to live and survive in the world today. Do you have any interest in learning how to survive and live without access to money? How can you use the tool at your disposal in the very best way possible?

As you learn new skills and make different decisions, it will produce benefits that impact generations in the future. You get to decide how to do the most good for yourself, your family, and the people around you, which will teach others a new way to live.

Automate

Automating, creating systems, and reducing the choices you need allows you to focus your mind when it's most important. Take steps to automate your finances. Whether it's reducing debt, paying your monthly expenses, creating a cash flow system, or generating financial freedom, set up everything on autopilot. Set it and forget it. When you automate, it reduces the decisions that you need to make. The fewer decisions you need to make, the better your finances will be in the long term. One of the first things to automate in your quest for great habits around money will be to create a reserve account to protect you from destruction with emergencies or moments of weakness.

Suppose you have many debts, and paying those debts take up much of your income. It will help reduce the emotional negativity in your life when you set up an automatic repayment plan. That way, you won't have to think about debt, lack of money, or who to pay first when there isn't enough money to go around. If you tend to make impulse purchases or squander your money on things you don't need, it may leave your family living paycheck to paycheck.

- Leave your debit and credit cards at home.
- Set yourself a daily, weekly, or monthly limit and get enough cash to cover that time frame.
- Start wherever you are and work your way up to longer and longer time frames.
- If you can trust yourself for only one day, carry just enough cash to get you through that day.
- Lower the number of good decisions you need to make each day.
- Lessen the chances for discouragement from spending part of your monthly budget.

How well do you make good financial choices when shopping for groceries on an empty stomach? How difficult is it when your kids are hungry? It can be a challenging experience. I bet you make better choices when you are grocery shopping on a full belly. Do whatever it takes to make yourself successful. Reach out to someone who can help guide your decisions, give an objective opinion, and get the perspective of someone who knows finances.

Two factors can help you attain success:

1. **Self-discipline**

    A lack of discipline to yourself can become a habit where you consistently don't follow through on what you tell yourself you are going to do. The easiest person to disappoint is ourselves. **Discipline to self is your ability to set limits and honor them.** When you lack self-discipline, it creates no limit for making bad choices for yourself. Overeating, overspending, and doing anything to excess can become more challenging to control. <u>When you don't honor your decision to do something beneficial for yourself, such as getting up on time, exercising, or</u>

working toward a particular achievement, it can feel that your life is out of your control.

2. **Reduced decision-making**

The term "decision fatigue," originally coined by Roy F. Baumeister, explains the emotional and mental strain we feel after making too many decisions. Decision fatigue happens when you have a reduced ability or capacity to make good choices. It can occur throughout the day or during a highly stressful or demanding period in your life. The more decisions you must make will limit your decision-making capacity. Set up a system for optimal success and reduce the number of decisions you must make. It will help you avoid making bad decisions.

Reserves

A proper foundation is necessary for anything built for longevity and retention. It's your security. What you build will not collapse when you invest the energy and resources to have a great foundation in place. A good foundation is necessary for relationships, business, finances, or agriculture. The foundation of your finances is the ability to withstand anything that goes wrong, emergencies, economic strain, stress, illness, unexpected death, or loss of income.

The total reserves you have in place will dictate how long your internal financial system can continue without any additional income. Reserves are never a waste of money. Your money is not sitting around doing nothing when categorized as reserves because it is your solid foundation for whatever happens in your life. You will learn there are many options for places to store reserves. Having a reserve account in savings where it earns very little is better than not having any reserves at all.

Calculate how long your reserves will last without any income by dividing the total amount of reserves held by the

total amount of monthly payments and expenses. That will give you the number of months you can continue to pay your bills without any income, payments, or disbursements received. It is important to know the number of months you can live or exist without any income to mitigate your risk of insolvency.

Common excuses not to hold reserves include: "My money is just sitting there"; "It's not making anything"; or "I should do something good with that money." Those excuses sound like limiting beliefs and scarcity. If that's your reason not to hold reserves, maybe you don't believe you are worth having money or have a limiting belief that you don't deserve money.

You are worth having money. Your limiting belief will keep you exactly where you are right now unless you figure out the internal belief and how it is stopping you. You are worth having security in your life. Let go of the ideas someone else gave you and set your intention for a new destination. You are worth it.

The most common recommendation is to start your reserves with three months of expenses. You will probably find that it doesn't feel like enough when you get that amount saved. Six to twelve months will give you huge confidence that you can withstand any economic downturn or employment lapse that comes your way.

Mitigate Risk

Contrary to the narrative of traditional investment advice, you do not need to take on more risks to achieve a greater return. It is common for sophisticated investors never to accept another person's risk. Banks make a practice of limiting risk by ensuring you pay ten to thirty percent of the price as a down payment. The higher the down payment typically means the bank calculates greater risk for the loan. You can reduce risk through various ways in real estate and notes. When you understand this concept, you will have a greater capacity to borrow money and negotiate with lenders.

"Both"

As children, we want everything all the time. Since we can't discipline, control, or ration ourselves, parents will begin to give choices. Often, it is two choices: "Do you want the blue one or a red one?" Maybe you were at your mom's friend's house, and she had brownies and apple pie. You never had brownies or apple pie at your house, and you begin to pile up a plate full of sweet goodness. Quickly, your embarrassed mom swoops in to remove the pile and says, "You can't have everything you want." Hmmm, I can't have everything I want? Thus begins the story and belief system that you can have only this or that, one or the other. Never both.

What if you could erase the past and choose both? You can have a brownie and a slice of apple pie. We don't always have to live in the moment of either/or—sometimes choosing both is the best answer. Do you want to enjoy your career and have a great family? Do you want to love your job and take amazing vacations? When you feel the weight of a big decision weighing on you or possibly something doesn't feel right or fit your intention and purpose, think about how you could implement "both" scenarios.

> A scarcity mindset believes that money, resources, opportunities, or successes are limited and must be taken from someone else to receive it for themselves.

Abundance Thinking versus Scarcity Mindset

Jealousy and competition come into play with a scarcity mindset. It isn't pleasant to believe you need to take something from someone else to get it for yourself. It requires you to justify why you are more worthy than the other person so you can get it for yourself. I do not want the weight of deciding whether I am more worthy or not. It is best if we both can have what we want.

Do you worry about running out of something or not having enough? Does it bother you to let one of your friends know that you have spent time with another friend? Are you concerned that you will upset your spouse if you spend time with other people and don't include him? All of these thoughts can come from a scarcity mindset. There isn't enough of me or enough love inside of me to go around.

When you believe "there isn't enough," it affects what you think about most. "We can't afford this, we can't pay that, we can't do that because it costs too much," and the list goes on and on with your mind and mouth proclaiming scarcity in your life. You spend so much energy thinking about how there is not enough money to affect your entire life. Therefore, money is what you think about most.

What if you had not eaten for six days? How much time would you spend thinking about food? Everything would remind you of food. You might dream about having the best dinner imaginable with wonderful dessert and more food than you could eat in one sitting. It's the same with money when you are deprived or feel you don't have enough.

When you believe you don't have enough, you want more, and more, and more. All you think about is money because your body and mind are in deprivation mode. When a bill comes in the mail, what is the first thing that comes to your mind? "Not another bill." "I can't pay for this." "I don't have enough money." What about your paycheck? "It's never enough." "I wish I made more money." What goes through your mind when your kids come to you for money? More importantly, what do you say to them? "All you want from me is money." "Do you think I'm made of money?" "We can't afford that." And the list goes on.

Such situations arise throughout the day, and you react unconsciously. Recognize the thoughts in your head and what results you create in your life. What thought patterns are you teaching your kids? You are writing on their slate forever. Are you teaching them to think scarcity or abundance? Abundance perpetuates itself the same way by producing more and more of what you are thinking. Thoughts of abundance means you believe plenty of resources are availableto you and your job is to receive yours.

Future Freedom

When you achieve freedom and experience abundance, you will want to ensure that this way of living follows you throughout your entire lifetime. Our society, with good intentions, has set up a system that rewards fiscal behavior that saves money from today to live on or spend tomorrow. A few fundamental flaws in that system may cause us to not realize until it's too late to make any changes.

We learn from the experts to put off what we want today for what we will need tomorrow. Living your life of abundance teaches you to live your life today and plan for sustainability tomorrow. Recovering can be challenging if you miss addressing these concepts during future planning conversations. It is often beneficial to address them early. These are small flaws in the system, and unfortunately, we won't realize until it is too late to make adjustments.

Fundamental Flaws

Inflation: The first flaw is not accounting for inflation. Things continue to cost more in the future than they do today. Even though inflation had been at historic lows for a long time, prices for goods and services and the cost of living have continued to rise.

We are now experiencing rapid jumps in inflation during the COVID economy, and many of us have never lived as adults during inflationary periods. Houses, rent, food, gas, clothing, and literally all goods and services are currently increasing. The last figure I heard was six percent inflation over the past year. It is mildly annoying now, and most of us have not felt the full effects of inflation yet. Many of us are on the positive side of inflation, where we have more money to spend from the stimulus payments, COVID loans, and the surging economy, and we haven't felt the financial crimp of price increases.

Inflation happens even when we aren't watching it; therefore, it is best to calculate it in your planning.

You won't need as much when you get older: Many experts suggest we won't need as much to live on as we get older. Research has shown as the average age of a country's population increases, inflation will go down slightly as we require less "stuff" to live. Many countries have reported a decrease in overall inflation as the population ages. Babies require much more money to grow into adulthood than we need as adults. Once the first apartment, newly married, and first baby phases pass, we need to buy fewer things that we already own.

There are a few areas where we will see decreases, such as not eating as much when we get older, so our food costs might decrease. We may eventually tire of travel and be content to spend less time and money on concerts or amusement parks. Ultimately, though, your cost for care in medical expenses, prescription drugs, and help to maintain your home or physical independence will increase and overtake any of the small savings you calculated. The challenge becomes how to increase your income, or will you decrease elsewhere?

Taxes: Another flaw in traditional thinking is that you will pay fewer taxes as you get older. That is a historically false statement. Mathematically, you will likely pay as much or more in taxes as you get older unless or until you have a very small income.

The primary reason your taxes don't decrease is that we often lose tax deductions and exemptions as we get older. Dependents go away and become tax-paying citizens. Mortgages front-load interest. Therefore, as your balance decreases, you will have less and less mortgage interest to deduct. Business owners and independent contractors often begin to slow down and cut back, minimizing many business deductions available during the growth phase.

These are all truths you will experience, and we haven't discussed potential tax rate increases yet. Your best plan for minimizing taxes as you get older will be to plan now for available tax deductions, such as real estate tax advantages that continue well into retirement. Find a great tax planning professional and get advice for now and well into retirement. It is always beneficial to have an excellent tax planning professional on your team.

Healthcare expenses and cost of insurance: Healthcare insurance has continued to rise despite attempts and promises to fix it. Although there is much improvement in insurance availability, it simply costs more to insure someone older. The current system charges us more as our health decreases and age increases. As our age and costs increase, we are more likely to eliminate a traditional employer, further increasing our expenses.

It is a flaw in the system for us to be told or led to believe that we will need less money when we get older. Don't believe anyone who tries to convince you of that. You worked hard your entire life for your money. You deserve an opportunity to live your life without being enslaved to an employer or a small fixed budget. You will not need less to live on in retirement, your taxes won't likely decrease, and you will continue desiring to live a great life.

Capital gains taxes: This is a big expense that often gets missed in future planning. It can be one of the most detrimental taxes to our older generation. The percentages fluctuate regularly without anyone understanding how it will affect one's future or parents and grandparents. Being in real estate, I have had an opportunity to learn how capital gains taxes can destroy finances for some individuals and the misunderstanding in planning for them.

The biggest concern is how people lose hope when capital gains taxes become evident on the sale of real estate they have owned for decades. I am sad to understand how detrimental it affects the older generation. It takes planning, education, and access to a great tax professional to eliminate the negative effects of misunderstanding capital gains taxes.

The catalyst to understanding capital gains on real estate started when a friend attempted to help a widow on a fixed income by buying part of her primary residence and land. Her mortgage payment was half of her monthly budget, and prices for goods and services increased rapidly. The widow wanted to live out her last years independently and desired to move into a smaller home that needed some updating and repairs. Because of capital gains, she believed that selling her home would not net enough cash to make the repairs and ease the strain on her budget.

This woman and her husband had lived the American dream, acquired hundreds of acres of the most beautiful land, and made all their payments. Unfortunately, capital gains taxes and a real estate commission would eliminate most of the money she would get from the sale. Capital gains taxes are not just a tax on the wealthy; it is a tax on the most dedicated and hardworking Americans. Here are a few specifics for planning how to navigate capital gains taxes:

- You get up to $250,000 without being taxed on your personal residence when you meet the living requirements of twenty-four out of the previous sixty months.
- Married filing jointly can claim up to $500,000 in tax exemptions. If you are a surviving spouse, you will receive the step-up value at the date of death for your spouse and will subsequently own 100 percent of the asset instead of 50 percent of the asset when your spouse was alive.

- You cannot ever claim this exemption on second residences, vacation homes, rental property, or property used for business.
- The capital gains tax calculation will recapture depreciation you previously claimed and is not based on the simple formula of what you paid versus what you received at the sale.
- The depreciation deductions phase out at certain income levels, so please talk to a very good tax professional.

Decreasing asset retirement: The biggest flaw and limitation of the traditional retirement planning industry is its structure based on a decreasing asset. We work our entire lives to build up a pile of money in accounts the government has made available to us. The flaw is that we believe if we do what they tell us to do, we will be fine.

Many retirement specialists who look highly successful from the outside have accumulated massive amounts of real estate without your knowledge. They do not advertise it in their marketing information. Holding my investment licenses allowed me the opportunity to learn that information by accident. If investing in the traditional market is that lucrative and solves your retirement problems, why are they investing time and money buying real estate?

It is a major flaw not to consider how a decreasing amount in your retirement accounts affects your retirement disbursements. Balances will decrease in value as you take money out. The government also requires you to pay taxes on certain portions and accounts. The sad news is that you will not keep up with inflation in a decreasing asset because you will need increases in your income as time progresses to cover rising costs. When you need your value to be the highest is when the value will be the least. As you begin to pull money out of your accounts to use during retirement, the expectation is that you will only pull out the earnings from the account. The truth is that every time you make a withdrawl, some of your shares will be sold and you will have fewer shares. Mathematically it is impossible to keep all of your original asset intact until the day you die.

Experts used to recommend four percent as the safe amount to deduct per year from your account to avoid reducing your original balance. Now, companies have proven the magic percentage is closer to two and one-half percent. You will be pulling some of the principal out during your retirement, which means your 2.5 percent withdrawal amount will need to be less, or you will continue pulling more and more of the principal out of your account, making it a decreasing asset. Inflation and taxes also increase your need to withdraw more money, which further compounds your decreasing asset challenges.

10

Live Your Life with Strength

Then make my joy complete by being like-minded,
having the same love, being one in spirit and of one mind.
(Philippians 2:2, NIV)

IF YOU WANT to perform better than the masses and achieve results from your efforts, read on. Much of what we are taught about finances tends to keep us stuck where we are and keeps us dependent on the choices of our employer, the government, or a paycheck. There is a better way to live and plan for your future. When you are intentional about using your time and your paycheck toward creating abundance in your life, you will find much greater freedom and strength in your finances. That is great motivation to keep moving forward.

Forget everything you have been told or taught about money. Almost everyone agrees that we need better education on finances. Much of what is taught in schools or financial education programs do not teach you to get ahead. I want to see you live for more, continue to grow, and bear good fruit.

I have compiled a list of powerful financial concepts to help you gain strength and abundance in your personal and business finances. Each topic contains an introduction to the idea that will aid in your understanding of it. When I started on my journey to learn and understand the concepts of wealth, abundance, and real estate, I did not know any of these beyond hearing someone mention a few of them in a conversation. I could not participate with any insight or understanding.

Your strength will come from continuing to learn, grow, understand, and implement these strategies little by little. Take your time, ask questions, don't give up if you don't understand, and slowly implement something you learn here that might work for you.

Powerful Financial Concepts

- **Leverage**

    Leverage uses borrowed money to purchase something, such as real estate or any asset that provides cash flow. Bank loans are leverage. Borrowing leveraged money from banks is the most prevalent, and it is often the first and only option we think to use. You can use leveraged funds from insurance companies, individuals, funds, groups, and anyone or place that is willing to lend on your asset. This allows you to purchase a higher-priced asset by using a small amount of your money and leveraging that with a large amount of someone else's money. It can greatly increase the amount of revenue you bring in, although you must balance the additional cost of the debt when you borrow money.

    When you use bank money to purchase a cash-flowing asset, the bank accepts the risk of inflation or their money having less purchasing power in the future. Banks also use leveraged funds to offset their inflation risk and fractional reserve lending to enhance the returns they get. Using leveraged money from a bank loan provides greater returns for you, the ability to purchase more, potentially bigger cash flow, and a hedge against inflation.

- **Velocity**

    The velocity of money is a measurement of the rate at which money is exchanged in the economy. Simply put, velocity is the number of times that a dollar moves from one entity or person to another.

Reading the story of the Stranger and the $100 bill the first time opened my eyes to something I intrinsically knew and didn't understand. Most simply, it explains how the economy keeps growing and why we feel rich in good times and sluggish when the economy is slow. The speed that money changes hands makes all the difference in how we perceive the economy is doing. It also explains why the great recession felt its effects so strongly after the 2008 crash. Banks stopped lending, people stopped buying, renters stopped renting, and money was stagnant in our economy.

A bald-headed, bearded stranger stopped at a small-town hotel to see if they had any rooms. He asked the clerk if he could check out the rooms first, and in good faith, he left a $100 bill—a deposit of sorts— with the hotel owner.

While the stranger went to look at the room, the hotel owner ran next door to pay his grocery bill.

The grocery store owner went across the street to pay one of his suppliers for his overdue balance.

The supplier quickly used the $100 to pay off his co-op bill.

The co-op guy ran it across the street to pay the local hooker who had taken up residence in the hotel mentioned above.

The hooker ran it downstairs to pay her hotel bill just ahead of the returning traveler, who picked the $100 bill up off the counter and said the rooms were not satisfactory as he walked away.

The question for you is, are all of those debts paid? If you ask any one of those people, they will say, yes, the debt is paid. Think about tax revenue in this scenario. How many times is the $100 taxed as ordinary income? The money will continue to be in circulation, earning more money, incurring more taxation. As long as money moves from person to person, we will continue to have a strong economy.

There are a few important aspects of velocity. The first thing to notice in the above parable is a fundamental understanding of abundance. Simply put, $100 in this story turned into $600 without the need to invest any additional time or effort. It's in the very nature of money to multiply.

You might also note that everyone in the parable seemed to feel richer, more abundant, and more hopeful when money was changing hands quickly. If you have ever lived in a small town without many job opportunities, you will recognize the feeling of slow velocity. The extremely slow velocity of money was also a big factor after the great recession period of 2007 to 2009. When banks quit lending money, very few people could get a loan. People who currently had loans couldn't qualify for another one. Everything slowed down. The sale of real estate halted without loans available, and money had a much longer turnover time. We experienced fewer jobs, minimal travel, fewer renters, and fewer qualified home buyers. All of these factors and more hindered the speed or velocity of money. When money is readily available to borrow, we feel more abundant, and the velocity increases.

The most important aspect of velocity in your personal situation is how quickly you can use the same money to make more money. The parable showed the same money multiplying from person to person. You can also use velocity for yourself and your business. The quicker that money changes hands, the more times the same money can produce more. Velocity is why a certificate of deposit at the bank is often not the best investment choice for cash. The interest rate is not the only factor to consider because CDs are locked in place for many years. During that time, the bank is leveraging your money to capture the effects of velocity in short-term loans, and they can multiply the number of loans they make with the same leveraged funds. Investing in a CD will give banks the power to use velocity at a high level, not you.

- **Arbitrage**

  Arbitrage takes advantage of a price difference between two or more markets and creates an acceptable agreement for all parties, capitalizing upon the imbalance and making a profit. This strategy creates abundance. It is multiplication, and it uses "both" to the very best.

  I have a house rented to a nonprofit. We had some conversations about how the nonprofit would like to own real estate to create income and become sustainable. We discussed the inherent risks of owning real estate, including vacancy, minimal cash flow, or unexpected repair costs. I was concerned the nonprofit would not experience desired financial security with the additional risk.

  As the owner, I stressed about a potential canceled lease, an unexpected vacancy, and costly repairs. I wanted more security with a good rental agreement, and they wanted to eliminate the liability of rent and utilities in their annual budget. It made sense that the nonprofit should rent to their tenants for more than they were paying for their lease. That is called arbitrage, and they could charge enough to cover rent, utility expenses, and potential vacancies. The nonprofit was taking on the risk of signing a lease in their desire to teach people how to live financially responsible lives. They could be fiscally responsible by covering their risk and retaining financial stability. It was a win/win scenario for everyone.

- **Tax Reduction and Elimination**

  The tax code incentivizes people to do what the government prefers and keeps the economy going. You have a choice to follow the rules to improve your current and future financial situation. It is in your best interest to learn the laws of the tax code and how you can best use them to benefit your family.

  Since the economy feels more robust as the velocity of money increases, the government will do whatever is necessary to keep the economy moving. It's evident as it protects certain industries and makes payments to specific people. The government creates rules that reward behavior they want to continue and de-incentivize people for doing what they prefer to cease. An example is a change in the tax code during COVID that made 100 percent of meal expenses deductible. Previously, the government had amended the tax code to reduce the deduction to 50 percent on restaurant bills. During COVID, an amendment to the tax code again allowed restaurant bills to be 100 percent deductible as a business expense. It was a way to boost the hurting restaurant industry.

  The government wants people to provide jobs through business and to buy and sell real estate because both offer a large avenue for money to change hands quickly. It is best to know what the government rewards through the tax code and use it to enhance and retain your wealth.

- **Depreciation**

  Depreciation is a part of the accounting process for large assets purchased for business purposes. Depreciation can be taken on machinery, real estate, equipment, etc. Individuals can use it for real estate purchased specifically for investments or business, but not for personal use. The investment has to be depreciated over time except in the case of certain tax amendments.

  You can use depreciation to lower your taxable income, and it is one of the best options available to retain and enhance wealth in the United States. There are many rules and regulations to follow to use it correctly. It will benefit you greatly when you understand and implement this in your finances. You will want to enlist a good CPA when using high-end tax strategies. It is up to you to learn the rules to manage how your CPA is working on your behalf.

- **The Vault**

  The vault is a place to park cash that offers a steady return with the ability to access your money for investing or emergency expenses. This strategy uses a specially crafted insurance policy that is super funded to maximize available cash and produce greater returns that compound tax-free. This strategy is a great example of "both/and" multiplication because your money can earn returns in more than one way.

  People refer to the vault as cash flow banking and many other names. It allows you to become the bank and to create leverage with your own money. It can be especially beneficial when complementing real estate, holding reserves, managing business resources, leaving a legacy, handling family banking, and administering wealth retention and enhancement strategies.

- **Mortgage Acceleration**

  Mortgage acceleration is best when you can pay down your loan faster without increased payments or less cash on hand. It gives you the benefits of "both/and." Many people dream of paying down their mortgages early. It is a large payment in their monthly budget. The time frame to eliminate your mortgage bill is typically decades into the future.

  Typical mortgage acceleration plans utilize three strategies:

  1. Pay extra monthly toward your mortgage.
  2. Pay bi-weekly, resulting in an extra half-payment twice per year.
  3. Make a lump-sum payment with cash on hand.

  A high-end strategy pairs the sweep and HELOC strategies to pay down your mortgage faster without using additional cash per month AND not taking money out of your reserves or investable cash. If your goal is to enhance and retain your wealth and maximize your efforts, it may not be best to use cash on hand in these three strategies to pay down your mortgage. I have known about this for years and am slow to adopt changes in our finances. We are currently beginning this process, and I will be excited to share the outcome with everyone.

- **The Family Banking System**

  The Family Banking System is a way for families or businesses to use their own capital for financing. In the simplest form, it means that you have money in an account at a bank or anywhere highly liquid that is available for your family members to borrow. Family banking is an easy strategy to implement, and it works with kids at any age. Family Banking often pairs protection with enhanced wealth creation strategies to establish a system that builds and maintains generational wealth. The process can continually be improved upon and enhanced as your financial needs and understanding grow.

The steps will be: 1) set money aside in the family bank, and 2) decide how and when to add money to the bank. When a family member requests a loan, you will decide whether or not to approve the request as a group or bank board and if the terms need to be changed or adjusted. Family banking teaches skills that the entire family needs to learn, such as risk mitigation, autonomy, freedom, and control of monetary resources. It's a great way for kids to understand the power of borrowing, and it can be used as a loan to start a small business.

My twelve-year-old son wanted to buy a program to play video games online. His idea was to ask for a twenty-dollar loan, and everyone agreed to approve it. I wondered how he would pay for it since he tends to spend money faster than he receives it. When he finally had approval to buy, the price had gone up by five dollars, and he had to renegotiate the loan. He was worried that he would forget to make his loan payment that was due on a date when we would be out of town, and he learned a valuable life lesson: *You can pay early but not late.* I was impressed with his responsibility, and he is now the most experienced financially of our three kids.

- **LOC/HELOC Sweep**

  A sweep account uses a line of credit with interest calculated as an average daily balance. You sweep discretionary money into the account for as many days as possible, lowering your average daily balance and your monthly payment. Discretionary money sweeps back and forth before using it to pay bills or payments. The lag time between payments saves you interest and cash out of pocket.

It's an advanced strategy requiring further research. A coach is beneficial to navigate learning this strategy and eliminating risk. I had advanced coaching when learning this and other high-end strategies. We had the chance to use this strategy to buy a cash-flowing asset, and it was a fantastic alternative to using cash on hand. We continued to keep the money in reserves that would have paid for the purchase, further mitigating risk. I sweep rent from a rental property into the account until it sweeps back to pay the mortgage payment, and the quarterly payments from the asset provide further balance reductions.

- **Overnight Investment Sweep**

   An overnight sweep takes receivables from the day and sweeps them into a short-term investment account overnight that sweeps back in the morning. The money is used for short-term investments and is swept back into the business's account at the beginning of the next day to increase short-term returns and maximize the return and value of your cash inflow.

- **Cash on Cash Return**

   Cash on cash return will tell you the amount of return you are making based on your investment in any asset. It is the most accurate calculation to compare investments with each other. The cash-on-cash return is the actual return on your money and not the return related to the investment. Using leveraged funds and less money down strategies can drastically increase your cash on cash return.

$$\text{Cash on Cash Return} = \frac{\text{Yearly Cash Flow}}{\text{Total Cash Invested}}$$

The top number is the amount you estimate receiving every year from the investment. The bottom number is the amount of money you contributed for your ownership.

Example: When you receive $4,500 every quarter, that is $18,000 yearly cash flow. You will divide your yearly cash flow from the total investment of $110,000 to get your cash on cash return. 18,000/110,000=.163636 or 16.3% cash on cash return.

That means 16 percent of your initial investment is returned to you every year, and all of your money will be returned in approximately six and one-half years. Once your principal is paid back, the return on your money will be infinite, and you will be earning money with zero money invested.

- **Seed Money**
  Seed money is the investment you make in cash to begin your asset portfolio or business venture. The primary objective of seed money is to continue to multiply it the way one seed planted in the ground will produce a much larger harvest. Your goal will be to continue to multiply your seed money and use velocity to invest the same money in more, bigger, or higher cash-flowing properties.
  In 2010, I purchased my first rental property. The banks were no longer lending with reckless abandon, and I could not find anyone to lend me money without putting 20 percent down in cash. I invested what was necessary and did not learn other buying strategies for quite some time. I felt as if I had lost the battle by giving in to pay 20

percent down. At the time, it felt that I would never get that money back. It became clear that although we had sacrificed a large sum of money upfront, the investment increased our returns as time went on and allowed us the opportunity to have higher returns and cash flow.

When we sold that investment, the money we would have received at closing went into a 1031 exchange, and we used all of that money for our downpayment on another investment property. The new property was updated and commanded top rental rates at the time. Our cash flow was much higher with the new property, and we did not add any additional cash for the investment. The seed money allowed us to get into bigger investments that produced greater cash flow later.

- **1031 Exchanges**

  A 1031 exchange is a strategy that uses tax code section 1031, which allows people to exchange one property for another and postpone paying taxes on the gain. The 1031 exchange rolls the sale proceeds of one property into another to avoid paying taxes on the asset's appreciation and depreciation deducted during ownership.

  Initiating a 1031 exchange must be done when you sell the investment property and before closing. You will hire a third-party administrator who controls the money until your subsequent purchase. In a 1031 exchange, you will not have access to any money and must pay taxes on anything that does not get rolled into the next purchase. If you take possession of the funds at closing, you will have lost any opportunity to do an exchange.

  There are extremely specific rules in 1031 exchanges. Please consult someone with experience to help you and consult real estate agents who have previously done exchanges for themselves or clients.

- **Little and No-Money-Down Strategies**

  Little or no money-down means you invest little or none of your own money to purchase an investment. You will acquire cash-flowing assets without depleting your current cash or reserves. Leveraging is often a necessary part of this strategy, and the down payment can be structured creatively. You may also take ownership through various owner-finance scenarios or subject-to, which takes over another person's mortgage.

  It's worth it to learn additional strategies to increase ownership quickly. Certain techniques can work better based on your goals, geographical location, and current market. Since there are many ways to implement these, it will be best to find a coach to teach you the best way for your situation, location, and preference.

- **Equity Stripping/Tax-Free Income**

  Equity stripping is an asset protection strategy that places debt on an asset, so it appears there is no equity available for a creditor or judgment. It can be an effective strategy for real estate and non-business assets when part of a well-thought-out strategy.

  A line of credit or home equity line of credit will show up as a lien and is simple to implement. You can refinance properties with low loan to values with traditional higher bank loans. The cash received is not taxable and can buy additional assets, be kept for reserves, or make updates to real estate. A high-end strategy uses an entity you own to create a lien on real property that you own individually or under a separate entity. A recorded lien will reduce the equity available on your property.

- **Self-Directed IRA**

  Self-directed IRAs are retirement accounts similar to a 401(k) that allow individuals to self-invest in non-traditional assets such as real estate, coins, art, etc. It can be awesome to control your own retirement money, and it certainly increases your access to capital while protecting the tax advantages of retirement accounts. A handful of self-directed IRA companies will help you navigate the process.

The learning curve is large, and it can be a slow process to access the money. The first time I tried to use an IRA to purchase a large asset, it didn't go well. Since then, I have learned how to navigate the rules of self-directed IRAs and have initiated dozens of asset-backed loans for real estate purchases. It can be an incredibly useful tool for your wealth enhancement and retention goals. Get help navigating the rules, regulations, and processes so you can gain the biggest benefit for your portfolio and learn the many ways you can invest IRA money.

- **Asset-Backed Lending**
  Asset-backed lending creates a loan, mortgage, or deed of trust collateralized with real property. It works similarly to how a bank works, except the lender is not a bank or regulated banking institution. In this scenario, you benefit from earning interest on your principal investment, tied to collateral from a real asset such as real estate. Interest rates are often higher than bank loans. Risk can be mitigated by decreasing the loan to value ratio and how many potential selling strategies are available.

- **Note Investing**
  Investing in a note is buying a mortgage. The note will have a number of payments remaining, and it will either be performing or non-performing. Performing means the payments are paid and up to date according to the terms. Non-performing means the mortgage holder is in arrears and not paying according to the terms. Buying

notes is purchasing a mortgage, loan, or deed of trust that someone created between the owner of an asset and a lender on the real property. The purchase price of a note will reflect a discount based on the number of payments remaining and the risk of the loan.

Community Is Key to Your Success

Freedom comes through the knowledge you gain and your relationships with others. When you find a community with similar thoughts and ideas, you will no longer be alone. A community of knowledgeable individuals will give you the courage to take action, help you notice blind spots or things you aren't seeing, and empower you through a network of like-minded individuals. That is empowering and encouraging, and it enables you to achieve the dreams in your heart.

Masterminds have become prevalent and important in the marketplace. The reason is because finding others on a similar path as you helps you move forward where others who are alone won't dare to go. You will not have the time or energy to learn everything that you need to learn to be successful on your move in any new direction without leveraging the skills and knowledge of people who have gone before you. It may take several attempts to find the best community for you. You will gain much knowledge and insight into what you like, what you don't like, and what you value most during the process.

A great first step you can take is to look for a local group, real estate investor group, networking group, or meetup that matches your goals. The REI Group in Springfield, Missouri, has given me the chance to build relationships with people in all phases of learning real estate investing. I have been fortunate to watch people succeed and blossom into what they dreamed they would become and to build relationships with others on a similar journey as I am on.

Other excellent ideas for finding a community of like-minded individuals are to join a mastermind group, start your own group, or join an investment club. Look online, in meetup, or on Facebook to see what is available. My husband joined a Facebook group called Physician Side-Gigs. It has been fun to hear about the young or motivated physicians focused on creating freedom rather than spending the rest of their lives dependent on the hospital system. You may also find subgroups similar to our Real Estate Investment Group, such as Beginners, Landlords, Women in Real Estate, Experts, and Finance Hackers.

I desire to make a profound change in the world through impact and giving. Therefore, my focus is specifically on building long-term wealth and creating freedom rather than having real estate become my full-time job. We have a mastermind called Freedom on YOUR Terms, and I have personally coached people to follow the dreams in their hearts and become who they are destined to become. I have a friend who coaches female business owners and several friends who coach in other areas. The best investment you can make is in yourself and your education. The more you learn, the more you will retain, and the more you will recognize that there are always new things to learn. Reading books, listening to podcasts, and finding your community will speed up your transformation and results in any direction you decide to go.

I have experienced hopelessness in my life. My goal at one time was merely to survive. Thankfully, God wasn't done with me yet. As I mentioned in the Prelude, a friend and I started a nonprofit called GRASP, which is focused on helping people experience transformational change in their lives. GRASP's goal is to encourage people to thrive and recognize the hope within themselves and to believe it's possible to thrive. When people see hope, it can begin a great and amazing transformation.

If you have read thus far, you must have many dreams inside of you, and we want to help you reach the desires of your heart and get to the place where you want to go. If you are looking to connect with a group of like-minded people who desire to thrive and believe they are destined for more in life, you can reach us by email at grasp.gives@gmail.com, check out our Facebook page at https://www.facebook.com/GiveforStrength, visit us on YouTube or Instagram, or view our website at www.grasp.gives.

We look forward to connecting with you.

11

Live Your Life a Blessing

And let us not grow weary of doing good,
for in due season we will reap if we do not give up.
So then, as we have opportunity, let us do good to everyone.
(Galatians 6:9–10, ESV)

YOU ARE BLESSED to be a blessing. The old idea of success being brought about by burning the candle at both ends, being on the go constantly, and sustaining yourself with coffee to make the most money and be the most important is no way to live. In that scenario, you can barely take care of your personal needs. It is impossible to think of other people when your needs aren't met, let alone be a blessing to them. The new version of success includes living a balanced life and meeting your needs to ensure the ability to pour into the lives of your family, customers, coworkers, and friends. You can have it all.

To be a blessing to others, you first need to take care of yourself. The emergency instructions on an airplane include putting your mask on first before helping others. If you pass out on the airplane, you are no good to anyone. That goes for all areas of life. You are significantly hindered in your capacity to be a blessing to others when you are stressed out and exhausted.

True long-term success will come for you when you have found your purpose and passion or at least have an idea and are working toward it. When you are focused on working toward your true gifts and passion in life, you can truly become a blessing to others. That is also when work no longer feels like work. You want to get up every day and do what makes you the happiest, and you will naturally provide the most value to others.

Success requires focus and effort. It means there might be times when your life is way out of whack, but it is manageable for a short period. Momentum can be your friend, and you may periodically need small bursts of insane activity to accomplish your goals. When the time is right, you will readjust yourself to a normal level because that lifestyle is ineffective long-term and is not a solution for success.

I once heard our pastor say, "The world of a stingy person gets smaller while the world of a generous person gets bigger." That has been my experience in life, and many of you may have experienced that as well. People did not get to know me when I was shy and reserved, and I did not have any close friends. As my ability to connect and share my story and words of encouragement grew, the number of great friendships grew as well.

God is looking for "channels," or people, to bless His people. Are you a person who wants more in your life so you can offer more to others? The world needs available people to be blessed to pour blessings onto others. The world needs generous people who can bless others who exist in a needy world.

Part of your passions and purpose will include giving away the gifts you have received to bless others the way you are greatly blessed. Blessings, like abundance, encompass more than money. You can bless others with your time, talents, resources, kind words, understanding, teaching, money, or anything else you can think up.

Some confusion about being blessed includes the belief that you must always give without expecting anything in return. Otherwise, you are not giving willingly and with a cheerful heart. You can give of what you have received. That does not necessarily mean you never receive a return from your gift or must always give it away for free. Recently, I heard someone speak about this topic. This man's gift is a service that is valuable to most people, including business owners, entrepreneurs, ministers, and nonprofits. He has chosen to sell his services at a high price point to businesses and entrepreneurs and offer his skill set to all ministers who request it, knowing they cannot pay his fee. He can give his talent away to ministers because he has a solid business model with qualified paying customers who want and need what he provides. That is "both/and." He has valuable and marketable skills, and he gets to give them away freely.

You can package the gift of your time, talents, and special expertise in a valuable way that adds value to others. You are blessed to be a blessing. Believe for yourself that it is not more honorable to give all that you have away without creating a livelihood for yourself. You can feel good about your ability to be generous with your talents and expertise and bless the lives of others with it.

Blessings and generosity always go out into the world and come back bigger than you gave. The attitude within your heart is the most important factor. I have experienced resentment in myself and others. That is not a good attitude within your heart. Often people feel resentment when they don't know how to ask for fair payment or feel compelled to give something away. Learning how to set values for your time and worth is the primary objective to eliminating resentment. You may have experienced an icky feeling when you see people being asked or are asked yourself to give money, time, or expertise. That is the first sign that the giver's heart is not right, and it will be beneficial to investigate the reason.

As you step into your place in the world, you will notice how little effort it takes you to do something you are truly gifted to do. That is a gift. It is where you bless others and your source of joy and happiness. You can share something that feels effortless to you but may be daunting, laborious work to someone else.

Good and Bad

Everything and all people have both good and bad. It is called integration, and it is a <u>strength of adulthood</u> when a person can hold both the good things and the bad things simultaneously. Everyone is good and a sinner. We can't have good without bad. There is no such world of one without the other.

The idea of integration does not seem that difficult to understand, yet many of us get stuck in our development process without learning it. When we were young, we thought our parents were great because we got to stay up late. Then our parents were bad because they punished us for throwing rocks after they told us not to. It is good that I enjoyed throwing rocks and watching them hit the ground. It is bad that I hit my sister in the head with a rock.

The same can be true of blessings. There can be both good and bad sides to a blessing. For example, you may get rewarded with a huge contract, and with it comes many late nights, multiple rounds of hiring, budget concerns, and the stress of not knowing how you will ever finish on time. Be willing to accept and experience both because you won't have good without acknowledging the bad. When you think about blessings and abundance, it means you are receiving something which may bring pains and growth along with it.

You might feel you do not deserve a blessing you received. It's difficult to understand, especially when it leaves you feeling unworthy. You are valuable and worthy. Notice the good feelings you are experiencing as you receive the blessing. Allow space for the good and resist the temptation to bring in a distracting statement, redirecting humor, or sarcasm. You are worthy of recognizing the good feelings that come up and opening your heart to accept your worthiness and share those blessings with others.

You can't give without first receiving. You can't spend without earning. You can't live in abundance without first experiencing want and then more than enough. Someone must first be the giver if anyone is to receive. These are never separate from each other.

You must have both the good and the bad, so how does that correlate to abundance and blessings? It correlates with regeneration, a natural and normal life cycle. The old dies and is cut away to allow more energy for the new to grow and flourish. Take a typical flowering plant, for example. The flowers bloom, and as time progresses, they die and turn brown. If the plant grows new flowers, it will require less time and energy to bloom after the old brown dead flowers are cut away. Giving up the old facilitates the best regeneration of a plant, which is true for people as well. If you accept and adopt new ways, you will first need to cut away and remove the old ways and mindset.

The second way it relates to abundance is the attitude within the giver's heart. What's in your heart can be good feelings and attitudes toward growth to flourish in thankfulness and appreciation. The feelings within you can also be bad attitudes that you want to cut away, such as jealousy or envy. When you understand that abundance is the good that comes out of the bad, you will appreciate the growth cycle and recognize that the bad is simply a season you need to get through to experience the good that is coming. The life cycle works in every situation within the universe.

When you are going through a rough period, remember that the plant willingly gives up its dead brown leaves with a great attitude for the cycle of growth that is coming. Soon you will also see many new colorful blossoms that will bloom in vibrant colors. You will find this phenomenon everywhere. Be willing to give up what you have, and you will be blessed with new. Giving with a joyful spirit will produce regeneration and abundance for everyone involved.

You Can't Save Yourself Wealthy

When you think closely about the ideas behind saving, there is no correlation to abundance. It seems to stem from the core belief of scarcity and holding on to something to keep it for self. My tendency has always been to be a habitual saver. I save everything and never use it out of fear it will disappear or break. Notice that there is no abundance mindset in that belief system. I chose to place a higher value on fear of loss over the potential for reward or gain for most of my life.

After many years of holding every dollar I could save, I noticed that I could never save myself wealthy. That didn't make any sense to me. Suppose I kept everything, then I should eventually have an abundance of what I saved. That never happened. One of my real estate mentors uses the phrase, "Savers are losers." That didn't make any sense to me either. How can the savers be losers if we are supposed to keep reserves and be wise with our money? It all comes down to velocity and multiplication. When you are holding on to your money, "saving it," you have zero speed or velocity, and you are stagnating. Velocity makes abundance, not saving or holding. The act of generosity, blessing, and velocity of money all seem to work together. Resources and money need to be used, not saved, to create more.

Ask for What You Need

Do you know what someone wants or needs without them asking for it? The same is true for your needs and desires. Nobody will know unless you reveal them. People often desire to do nice things for others and give them what they need. If you do not tell anyone what you need, someone else may guess and choose for you. That person may guess right, which could be a special treat for you, or he may guess wrong. A wrong guess doesn't hurt anyone if you are kind to the giver and not annoyed. You might feel a little bit let down, though. Wouldn't you prefer that you be given what you wanted? Do you think you would both be happier if everyone knew what would make you happy and feel special? It is truly a blessing to offer up your needs to another person. It allows someone to bless you in exactly the way you need it. When someone blesses you, it gives you more capacity to bless others.

So, I say to you: Ask and it will be given to you;
seek and you will find;
knock and the door will be opened to you.
For everyone who asks receives; the one who seeks finds;
and to the one who knocks, the door will be opened.
(Luke 11:9–10 ESV)

Availability to Receive

Many people will deny, say no thank you, refuse to accept, or turn away good things that come to them. Why do we choose not to accept what has been given to us? Do we reject gifts because we do not feel worthy? Is it because we think that we don't deserve it? Or is it because we believe doing without shows more humility and is more admirable?

You are blessed to be a blessing. You will continue to be blessed through your work, gifts, talents, and efforts. Accept the gifts you receive and the rewards for the value you provide to the world. Accept those gifts offered to you and bless others with continued generosity. You will be less available to be generous and do good deeds in the world if you are unwilling to accept gifts and financial rewards, especially if you believe that you do not deserve them.

You are blessed to be a blessing. Be available to receive the rewards bestowed upon you in all areas of your life. Treasure them up in your heart, be thankful for them, and give generously to others. When you are giving, loving, caring, happy, joyful, and thankful, people will be attracted to you and will want to be around you. Your abundance in all areas of life will be the magnet that attracts others to crave, understand, and experience what you have, which becomes a magnet for more abundance and blessings to show up in your life and the people who surround you.

12

Live Your Life of Generosity

But seek first the kingdom of God and his righteousness,
and all these things will be added to you.
(Matthew 6:33, ESV)

A GREAT DEFINITION of generosity is from the University of Notre Dame's Science of Generosity Project (Science of Generosity, n.d.). They define generosity as the virtue of giving good things to others freely and abundantly. You can be generous in many ways and with anything such as your time, money, possessions, attention, encouragement, joy, happiness, wisdom, expertise, or experience. The list could cover anything you can share with another person.

Most religions tell us to share our blessings with others generously. Giving is contagious, and as we give, more will be given back to us. You are blessed to be a blessing. Relationships are built through connecting and sharing. Offering your words of encouragement, a listening ear, or wisdom that you have gained is a way of being generous to others. You will never get all you desire for an abundant life without other people and generosity. Building relationships is a top priority. It will improve the happiness and satisfaction of your life, and your life is blessed through the blessings of others.

Giving is part of the human experience. Enjoy it. There has been an extensive culture of benevolence, philanthropy, and giving throughout history, which stems from religions and cultures worldwide. The word "philanthropy" (Word/Philanthropy, n.d.)

comes from the Greek word *philanthropia*, derived from *philos*, "a friend," and *anthropos*, "of mankind, people." That means the love of humanity, especially in deeds—a benefactor who works for the good of others.

Generosity comes from our hearts to give of ourselves and what we have to others in need or benefit from what we have received. As we dig a bit deeper into the core of giving, you will see a pattern of teachings within most of the world's largest religions.

The four largest religions in the world (Largest Religions in the World, n.d.) are, in order of size:

1. Christianity—has more than 2.3 billion followers.
2. Islam—the Muslim faith has 1.8 billion followers worldwide.
3. Hinduism—has 1.1 billion believers worldwide.
4. Buddhism—there are 500 million followers of its teaching.

The seventh-largest religion globally is Judaism, with fourteen million practicing Jews. The list does not include Mormonism or the church of Latter-Day Saints. It is unclear by reading the article where people who follow LDS were included or are excluded from the list. They may be listed within Christianity since the followers of LDS consider themselves members of a Christian church rather than a separate religion. I include LDS due to the specificity of their beliefs. Many people participate in the church, and I would like to include their beliefs in my research. The number of followers for LDS is sixteen million, making the Church of Latter-Day Saints the eighth largest religion in the world.

It comes from our hearts to give of ourselves to others in need and benefit from our generosity. You will notice a similarity and pattern of teachings within most of the world's largest religions as you read further into the core teachings about giving from each.

The Church of Latter-Day Saints (LDS)

Starting at the bottom of the list, the Church of Latter-Day Saints or Mormons believe in tithing, which means the tenth part. The church teaches that members will tithe or give the first ten percent of everything they have earned to God. December (Latter Day Saints, n.d.) is the month for tithing settlement where members sit with their bishops and declare themselves as a full tither, partial tither, or non-tither. The church requires that only full tithers may enter the temple. The end-of-the-year audit allows each member to settle his tithe on the year's earnings. Mormons are generous people and continue to practice generosity with the added benefit of accountability. The level to which the church holds its members accountable is likely one of the main reasons for their historically high giving rates.

Judaism

Jewish law commands its people do certain things that they believe God either wants or does not want His people to do. The mitzvah is a command, and one of the commands is to give. Therefore, Jewish giving is considered an obligation. It has eight graduated levels of charity (Eight-Levels-of-Charity, n.d.) that correspond to how much reward they get for their giving.

The first and greatest level of giving is to support a fellow Jew. It's the highest level of worthiness attached to an act of giving, and the level decreases with each lower level of giving. The lowest level in the command is to give unwillingly. Jewish doctrine says that God gave to us to give to others, and it is a standard Jewish practice to provide at least ten percent of your net income to charity. As you can see, Jewish culture has a deep connection to the heart of the person who is giving.

Buddhism

Giving in Buddhism is a gift of the heart and emphasizes an open-hand and open-heart orientation in life (Gift of the Heart—Giving in Buddhism, n.d.), which is essential to making spiritual progress. "Dana" is a universal virtue in Buddhism, which is said to be one of the most highly regarded virtues. The translation of "dana" is generosity or the attitude of giving. Buddhists believe dana will purify and transform the mind of the giver.

The range of a person's motivation while giving is most important in Buddhism. It is highly recognized that giving for the sake of getting something in return is less about giving and has fewer benefits to the giver. In contrast, transcendent giving is when the giver overcomes selfishness, and that attitude carries more importance. When giving a gift, the questions to ask oneself are: "What is my motivation?" and "What is the state of my heart and mind?"

Hinduism

In Hinduism, a religious duty is called a dharma. Every person has a dharma (Traditions of Giving in Hinduism, n.d.) toward family, society, the world, and all living things. As with Buddhism, the religious duty for giving is called dana. Dana or giving is an important part of one's religious duty. In Hindu cultures, giving extends beyond the temple. The duty toward family is one of the most important. The wealth that a person acquires is not for him or herself. It is for the welfare of the extended family and others, and that duty to one's own family is strong.

The tradition of giving in Hinduism acknowledges three types of giving (Traditions of Giving in Hinduism, n.d.). The first is giving without expectation in return or appreciation for the gift. That type of gift is a benefit to both the giver and receiver.

A gift that is given reluctantly and with expectation for something in return is the second type of giving. A gift given with reluctance will hurt both the giver and receiver. The last type of giving is a gift that is given without regard for the receiver's feelings or at the wrong time, which causes embarrassment to the recipient. They believe this type of giving hurts both the giver and the recipient.

Islam/Muslim

The religion of Islam has five pillars (Pluralism Files: The Five Pillars, n.d.), which are called the statements of faith. The third pillar is called zakat, which is compulsory giving. The standard is to give a portion of one's possessions, typically two and one-half percent of the annual wealth, given to local mosques or associations.

The ability to have "God Consciousness" (Pluralism Files: The Five Pillars, n.d.) and great discipline are increased by performing regular acts of worship within the five pillars. These common acts improve a person's attitude toward others. There is a heavy push to avoid selfishly using one's wealth and possessions. The zakat is a required annual payment made under Islamic law for certain property used for charitable and religious purposes. The zakat ensures justice in society, helps the needy, and promotes a greater vision.

Christianity

Christianity teaches and believes in tithing the first fruits of one's labor. Tithing is giving of the first ten percent of anything earned. Since God is the giver of everything, and all you have received belongs to God, the first ten percent is an offering of thanks and gratitude for all that you have. An offering is given for the benefit of glorifying God and continuing to grow His church.

There is very little accountability to the tithe in Christianity. All believers are free to decide what to give and how to give of themselves. God loves a cheerful giver. The goal is to provide ten percent from all earnings, yet there is a broad approach to the amounts and ways each person or family chooses to give.

Cultural Similarities

To summarize these various religions, several common perspectives appear among them. The first is that the _benefits of giving flow two ways, and giving provides more value to the one who is giving_. The giver becomes a happier, more joyful, and fruitful person. The internal benefit of the giver is what perpetuates the cycle of giving.

A typical response to giving is increased frequency and amount of giving. Givers feel good when they give, and they desire to repeat the good feelings experienced from giving. If a giver does not feel good after giving, he will cease to give further, and it would not be an act that has continued in every society and religion from the beginning of time.

Another commonality among these religions is that the _willingness to give is more important than the act of giving_. The giver's heart brings the most benefit to both the giver and the receiver. When someone gives with a sense of necessity, the gift is not as worthy of admiration, and it does not have a selfless giving spirit attached to it. The experience, or sense, of abundance, multiplication, and fruitfulness of the gift ceases without the giver's earnest desire to give of himself.

Money, abundance, resources, love, kindness, joy, and anything else you can think of do not survive in a vacuum. There must be a willingness to give and the velocity that comes from the repetition of giving and receiving. When giving ceases to be present, receiving will cease, and the cycle of abundance and multiplication will no longer exist.

When giving and hence receiving stops, everything stops. You cannot receive unless someone else gives. When you choose to do your part in giving, it will increase the velocity of giving. Receiving will undoubtedly increase abundance, multiplication, wealth accumulation, and enhancement around you. Abundance is created through giving and receiving and is perpetuated through the emotions felt through giving. People who have been blessed through the gifts of others often desire to give back what they have received. The cycle of abundance continues through giving and receiving.

Giving Goodness

Giving is good for you. One reason for the psychological boost you get from giving is that it shifts focus off yourself and onto the needs of others. You will gain a bigger perspective than yourself and your problems. What we focus on grows bigger and becomes most important. That can keep people stuck in a depressed state when they are laser-focused on themself and their problems. When a person begins to look outward, their issues and challenges become smaller and less significant. The new, bigger perspective can allow for noticing other possibilities and hoping for something different.

As an abundance-focused person, you probably are not depressed right now. Think about how much of a boost you can receive when your focus turns outward toward helping others. You are in control of your thoughts, feelings, and actions when you use this tool to shift your focus and drive your thoughts toward your goals and dreams.

Spend some time thinking about how you give currently. Maybe you have never thought about giving or do it only when you feel a twinge of guilt from a minister or nonprofit agency that asks for a donation. What kind of giving plan can you come up with that fits your life now, and what parameters do you want to set up for growth?

My life used to be full of guilt for not tithing, and I hated the "money" talk at church. After moving to Springfield, we started a church tour to find which congregation was a good fit. I will never forget the Sunday we visited a church, and it happened to be the "money" sermon. It would have been way too obvious to get up and leave at that moment. I had to fight to stay in my seat and listen. The car ride home was fun, "Can you believe we had to sit through that!?!" It was an entire Sunday full of guilt and shame.

Obviously, I would not be giving with the right heart or mind after listening to a sermon that left me feeling guilty and shameful. I felt condemned for not meeting the requirements or obligations expected of me. Now that I have made my giving plan and do so willingly, I feel joyful in our giving and look for opportunities to give more.

The percentage you give can be called tithing, dana, zakat, or whatever else you understand it to be. I used to think negatively about the rate. It seemed to be a demand or rule about how much I needed to give. When I reframed my thinking, it became clear how more giving equated to more earnings and blessings. It was a shift from scarcity to an abundance mindset when I could decide how many blessings I want to enjoy by establishing a goal for giving.

Every year, I increase our goal for donations. It is easy to keep track of our historical giving since we keep records for taxes.

The more you are giving, the more you are earning. Making that shift will provide you with an amazing new perspective on earning money, calculating what to charge for your products and services, and delivering value to others. How many people do you want to help this year? How much do you want to donate to your church or charity? When you look at it from this new perspective, you will feel energized and excited to get to work.

When I first started to learn and understand tithing, it was from reading the book *What is Prosperity and Does God Want You To Have It?* by Walter Hallam. The most impactful thing I learned from that book was the importance of starting where you are. You won't want to set an unattainable amount at your current income. My number, over twenty years ago, was $150 per month. It was not an unbearable number, yet it was a stretch to go from $0 to $150. Once we had decided upon that number, we took our first step to pay it one month. After that, it got much easier, and I continued with the same amount every month.

After we started regular giving, our minister had another "money talk." He went through the statistics of giving in our congregation. We lived in a working-class neighborhood and drove a short distance to a church in the top-income county around Kansas City. We were not making much money, but we continued giving our $150 per month. On the big screen at the front was a breakdown of the households who gave. It was broken down by where their monthly giving fit within the congregation. There were only a few families in the top category. The second-highest category of givers had between five and ten families with large monthly gifts. We were in the third-highest giving class of the entire congregation in the wealthiest county with our $150 per month donation. That was astounding to me. At that moment, I gave myself permission to let go of all guilt and shame around not giving enough. I stopped comparing myself to others without knowing all the facts. Everything that I give to someone else is enough, and it is a blessing to give.

Frequently people will experience a moment when God puts a number in their hearts. Undoubtedly, I have ignored or discounted that word most of my life. There are always doubts and questions. Was that really God? We doubt and second guess ourselves. I have analyzed myself out with logic many times. It is a growth experience, and God has grace for you on your journey.

Later in life, we adjusted and increased our giving to our church based on a new job and income levels. God placed a number on my heart that I wanted to honor. I also believed God wanted me to create a giving plan for our passive income, mostly from real estate and asset-backed lending. Next, God placed it in my heart that there wasn't a giving plan for my real estate earnings. That is tough since the income is infrequent and sporadic. I don't see any paystubs with those transactions, and the money gets directly deposited. It has proven difficult to track and continues to be a work in progress.

One of my passions is philanthropy, and my goal is to leave a legacy to my children and the generations that follow. It is important to me that I set up generational giving that will continue long after I am gone. We have set up a family foundation through my goals to implement the legacy of giving. A friend and I have also started a nonprofit with funds for giving and helping people learn to thrive. I have also participated with groups and nonprofits in our community. Decide what is important to you and your family.

Where do you want to make your impact and leave a legacy? My involvement started with the Community Foundation of the Ozarks, many grant committees, the Junior League, Rotary, multiple board positions, and several committees and fundraising drives for nonprofits in town. That level of involvement is certainly more than necessary, and at times it is a bit overwhelming, but it is what I want to do. It's is important to me. What's important to you?

Think about what you want and where you want to donate your precious time and resources. You have gifts that you can offer others, and you have a distinct passion inside your heart. Everything and anything you give freely of yourself is a gift and a blessing to others. Try it out if you have never made any donations to anyone. You may realize it's a passion of yours that's been waiting to get released into the world.

The Science behind Giving

Researchers and scientists have been studying for decades how people respond to giving. There is a large variety of research covering many topics around philanthropy. One topic that most agree upon is that a person's physical and emotional health is improved through benevolence—the benefits to giving begin with the release of endorphins.

Endorphins are opiate peptides produced in your body, influencing how neurotransmitters respond to sensations of pleasure and pain. That is much medical jargon to explain that endorphins give you that feel-good feeling or warm glow experience when you do something nice for someone else. Glands produce endorphins in your brain. They also go to work when you need pain relief.

When you do something that you enjoy, endorphins are released. Doing anything that you enjoy can prompt the release of endorphins such as dancing, having sex, eating great food, laughing, or being creative. A well-known release is often called the runners high. A similar experience to a runner's high can be produced from most exercises.

The feel-good sensation that you experience from endorphins gives you an emotional boost, leading to psychological responses that can have long-term health benefits. Therefore, the emotional responses to giving can create significant long-term health effects that equate to choosing not to smoke and not being obese.

In some studies, testing the brain has shown that when we do something nice for others, it stimulates dopamine releases in the brain. Volunteering your time can also produce significant health benefits, and research has shown that people volunteering to a worthy cause experience increases in happiness and joy. Many volunteers report feeling a greater quality of life, increased vitality, and higher self-esteem. The best part about happiness, joy, and higher self-esteem is how those feelings multiply as people share them with others. They become motivated to be more generous in the future.

Wired for Generosity

Although many people might suggest that humans are intrinsically selfish, studies show that it is our nature to be helpful and to give. In fact, humans are biologically wired for generosity. The drive for the common good can be seen throughout nature, such as in colonies of ants, hives of bees, packs of wolves, and herds of elephants. A dive into the habits of animals will typically show you patterns of behavior that may look odd or careless from our human perspective, yet will show the care and concern for each other's survival.

Why People Give

Beyond religious, social, and cultural connections, there are eight main forces (Weipking & Bekkers, 2010) that drive people to give. Researchers compiled eight mechanisms from over five hundred academic articles written on charitable giving. Their research involved scanning through all those articles. That is an impressive feat. The structure of their article is based on the question: *Why do people donate money to charitable organizations?*

Their research indicates the most important factors that dictate whether someone will donate. It also takes into consideration how much or how little they will give. Review this list and think about which items are most important to you if you are considering giving:

1. **Awareness:** I see an awareness of need.
2. **Solicitation:** Someone asked me to give.
3. **Impact:** I'm experiencing "tangible consequences" that have a monetary value and lead to a perceived benefit from my donation.
4. **Outcome:** I have a deep level of care for what the organization is doing and who they are helping.
5. **Reputation:** I perceive positive social consequences and an escalation of status after giving.
6. **Intangible Benefits:** I have increased pleasure, such as a boost in happiness, self-image, or confidence; and a decrease in pain such as guilt, disappointment, or discomfort.
7. **Values:** I believe the organization's work makes the world a better place.

The list above is just a glimpse into the details for each focus. As you consider getting more involved in organizations, consider whether the causes and organizations that interest you meet the following criteria:

- What is their mission, and how does it align with my core values?
- Do I trust how the organization will manage the funds I have entrusted to it?
- Will it use my resources to help people and expand programs directly?
- Can I see the impact they are making?
- Do I have a personal connection such as a family member or close friend who has been affected by what they do?
- Is this something that matters to me, and do I want to be part of it?
- Do you see this organization lasting for the long term? What is their public appearance? Where do you see them online or in your community?
- What do you want from this relationship? What are you looking for, and how will your need be met? Is it a mutual relationship with win/win outcomes, so you don't leave yourself out of the equation?
- Ask how and where the money is being used. You work hard for your resources, and you get to choose the impact you want to make with them.

Impact Is Key

The perceived impact that you make is key to the strength of your "giving high." The good news is that it is tied directly to the emotional reward you expect based on your anticipation and past experiences. In other words, *the emotional reward that you receive from making a gift will go as far as you can appreciate its impact.*

How do you perceive your gift will be received from the recipient? What matters most to you will be how you feel your contribution has made a positive difference. When you feel empathy toward the receiver of your donation, it will increase the reward and impact that you experience and will be directly attributed to your willingness to give.

The difference you feel will not be the same for everyone. Your focus may be on how the end recipient will be impacted, or your attention may be on the person who asked for the gift. The impact you experience may be for an entire country or group of people. None of these internal beliefs is right or wrong. They all have a place and make up the differences in why people give.

It seems that both are true. Humans are intrinsically selfish, and we are wired for generosity. It's the nature of the world we live in, and we must learn to live with the good and the bad.

13

Live Your Life of Impact

He that is faithful in a very little is faithful also in much:
and he that is unrighteous in a very little
is unrighteous also in much.
(Luke 16:10 ASV)

YOU WERE BORN for a reason. You were created to fulfill a purpose on this earth, and you are perfect just as you are. You are special, one-of-a-kind, unique. You are the only one who can do what you do. Your creation is intentional. God made you exactly correctly, and you are just the way He wanted you to be. There is a plan for you, and He can use you right now, just the way you are. Be thankful that you are God's masterpiece.

Living your life of impact will come naturally as you move from living in doubt, wonder, and uncertainty to finding your major definite aim. When you begin to live within your purpose and passion, you will become more confident. Knowing your direction and future will give you increasingly more belief in yourself. With more courage, your faith will grow too. Your courage, strength, confidence, conviction, and presence will impact the people around you, and you will naturally begin to have more impact within your sphere of influence.

Through their hard work and passion, influencers are people who have built a reputation for their wisdom and expertise. Influencers may build a sizeable network of trusted friends and acquaintances who respect their thoughts, ideas, and opinions. An influencer may also have a small and powerful group of followers. When an influencer is motivated, he can use his trust, respect, and influence to motivate others to act for the greater good, build momentum, and create great changes in the world.

Not everyone wants to be an influencer or has ever considered the possibility. A person can make an impact and be an influencer and either not know it or not recognize how it can be used in the world. You may have never considered the possibility of harnessing your impact and how you can use it for good.

1. You may not want to influence others or you may be completely uncomfortable with people listening to you, paying attention to what you are doing, emulating you, or influencing people in their decisions and direction.
2. You may have used your influence in the past to hurt others or bring harm, which causes guilt and shame for you.
3. You may be the leader of your group and allow the fun, adventure, and parties to be your only avenue of influence over your group.
4. You may want to have influence and not use your natural power to impact others.
5. You may not know where to direct your influence and impact because of your uncertainty of what you are passionate about.
6. You may feel guilt associated with your belief that you are taking advantage of people.

Having an impact is not about convincing people to do something they don't want to do. We all want to be part of a group. Everyone desires to be wanted, needed, and asked to participate. Being an influencer and making an impact are about leading people and inviting them to participate in something meaningful to you.

The great news is that God does not call the qualified; he qualifies the called. All your faults and screw-ups are an opportunity for God to use you. Little by little, God will transform your weaknesses into strengths. Adversity offers you a chance to grow, learn, and get better. As you grow, you become available to be used in a greater capacity.

What Level of Impact Do You Want to Make in This World?

As you grow through adversity, awareness, and openness to learning, your impact on those around you will grow as well. You can create an impact around you at a micro level or go all out and aim to become a person of influence at a meta level. Neither is better or more important than the other. The difference is solely in the type of relationships you influence and in your skill set and preferences.

You will impact and influence those in a small circle around you at a micro level. It could be your spouse, children, parents, and family members. Your coworkers and friends would all be considered at this level. When impacting at a macro level, you directly influence decision makers and those with influence over many others who either report to them or respond to their choices and decisions.

It is important to note the ripple effect of all influencers in every aspect of life. You are making a difference around you merely by your existence on this planet. What you do with your influence and how intentional you are about your impact is up to you. A mom can greatly impact her child, who may grow up to be the leader of a large corporation or a mailman who smiles at everyone. The minister at a big church can influence one person he never met, and a vlogger who is influencing the next generation can shift the direction of one young adult who may have never seen their potential. All these people are taking what they learned and using that to influence people for generations to come. One parent, supervisor, teacher, or scout leader can impact the entire world and not know it. Who is watching you today? Whose eyes are seeing how you show up in the world? You influence all who enter your circle, and they use that influence to influence others.

A kindergarten teacher or a little league coach can change one child's life who changes the world as an adult. It may be further generations down the line or one small change that yields to one small change that makes another small change. Have you heard of the Butterfly Effect? That is where the flapping of butterfly wings can make catastrophic weather changes around the world. We are all connected, so choose kindness and grace to make a difference where you are.

Bloom Where You Are Planted

Impact on Self: Start thinking about the impact you make on yourself. That may seem ridiculous to you at first; of course, you are making an impact on yourself. Often, we stop learning and striving for more as we grow older. We may fall into patterns that we learned growing up and use excuses, blame, or rationalization, and at times, we might still act a little childish to avoid taking responsibility. How long has it been since you went on an adventure or did something out of your comfort zone?

Impact on yourself may begin with trying something new or learning anything that interests you. Learning involves creating new pathways in your brain. Babies are adept at learning new skills. They can make as many as one million new neural connections every second. The formation of these new neural connections is called neuroplasticity.

The human brain is extremely efficient. Two things happen as we age. First, we don't need to learn as many new things. We have already done so much that there is less need for new neural pathways to be created. Second, when we come across something new, our brains will use previous neural pathways for something we are doing. Therefore, the brain's efficiency yields to a new skill that may not be completely new.

The skills that go along with learning will keep you feeling younger and keep you in shape to continue learning more and more. As you learn new skills, your brain will get faster at creating new neural pathways. Similar to working your muscles at the gym, your brain will get stronger and more efficient at learning new things again.

Take full responsibility for your life. Search out ways to help yourself grow in maturity and character. Seek out learning opportunities and take action. It may take time to find the right place to get the best answers. When you expect yourself to grow, you will begin to develop a deeper character structure and fully understand yourself. Your developing maturity will allow you to engage in meaningful adult relationships, and you will connect with others at a much deeper level.

Impact on Profession

What do you have to offer the world? Use the skills you have been given to impact people through your profession. Make an impact on your coworkers and your competitors. Your attitude and how you conduct business can make a huge impact on the world.

There are two sides to competition in business. On one side is scarcity thinking. That's when individuals believe they are competing for a limited number of buyers or clients. Your coworkers may say they are happy that you succeeded, but it doesn't feel as if they are happy for you. The underlying belief is that if you get more, they will get less. Consequently, they will believe the same thing when they get the big sale. Sometimes success may bring a little dread because they believe their win takes something away from you and everyone else.

This type of competition often doesn't feel good. People desire to be part of a team and know that someone has their back and that you are looking out for them. You can create impact by looking at competition from the viewpoint of abundance. Abundance thinking says, "I can be happy for your success because there is plenty for everyone," and "When you are successful, it means I can be successful, too." This mindset produces competition that benefits everyone and promotes all people succeeding. When you win, we all win.

In 2006, I had the opportunity to go to a Secrets of a Millionaire Mind seminar from T. Harv Eker after reading his book of the same name. He said one thing that has stuck with me for all these years. It forever changed how I view life and relate to others in work. He said, "Whatever your talent is, nobody else has been created to do what you do in exactly the way that you do it." He explained that your combination of talents and skills is unique. Even more than that, your ability to connect with a certain group of people is unique and special. You are the only person that can help those people in the exact way you do it. Be confident and move forward into what you are called to do, because you are the only person that can do what you do for some people in that way. It's important that you do what only you can do. You have an obligation to offer what you have for the world.

T. Harv Eker gave me permission to be me and pursue what I want to do in this life without fear of competition, fear of taking something away from someone else, and fear of upsetting someone who is doing something similar. I remember realizing that I never had to worry about competing with anyone again. I no longer had to be afraid of being a copycat or that I would be blamed for following someone else's plan. I didn't need to be afraid that I was taking something from someone else, because I am the only one who can offer what I do with my unique flair. There are more than enough opportunities for everyone.

That concept changed the way I view everything in the world. In the last six months, I have found several people I have never heard of presenting the same information that I am bringing to the world. Previously, it would have stopped me from moving forward, and I would have felt bad about myself. "Other people are already doing this" or "Everyone else does it better than I do.

Why should I even try?" Those self-defeating statements in my internal voice are scarcity and fear. When I noticed my discouragement the first time it happened, I remembered what T. Harv Eker had taught me all those years ago. Now, my perspective has been completely reframed, and it energizes me to see someone else doing the same thing. That means this information is needed, popular, and adds value to others, and people are willing to pay for it. It might not be needed or wanted if I am the only one presenting this information. I have also started to pay attention to how other people use and offer the information compared to my viewpoint and style. In that situation, it benefits me to either see where I can improve, see another perspective, or be more convicted in how I do things. We all win, and I can draw attention to how others present the same information, which builds further credibility.

You are the only one who can offer what you do in the exact way you offer it. Competition, scarcity, and jealousy are eliminated in your life when you adopt the belief that only you can offer "you" in this exact way to the world. If you are a physician, a dentist, a lawyer, or a hairstylist, you are the only one who can offer what you do in the exact right way for some people in the world. Are you a real estate agent, a plumber, a business owner, a fitness coach, or a car salesman? Whatever you do for your line of work, eliminate the belief that you are taking business from someone else to get it for yourself. People in the same field are not competing for the same business because you are all on the same team, and there is more than enough business for all of you. When there isn't enough business to support everyone, people will leave the field and look elsewhere. The real estate industry is a perfect example of supply and demand within the marketplace. The number of active real estate agents fluctuates greatly with the number of houses available to buy and sell and the number of buyers.

Impact on Others

One core need that everyone has is to connect with people. Even when someone has been severely injured or traumatized by others, the need does not go away; it is simply covered up, denied, and protected from further injury. We still need people in our lives, and we deeply desire a place to belong. Impact comes out of your connection with others. It stems from your likeness and affinity with other people. One of the greatest forms of flattery is mimicking someone. Since childhood, it has bothered me when children get bullied for copying and following along with the crowd. (I must have had a traumatic experience with this that I don't recall)

We all want to belong. We all want to be special and for our life to matter to someone. Adolescence is about figuring out who you are and trying new things. It's about finding and belonging to your group. Everyone needs to belong, connect to one's family, and build relationships with friends. We need connections. When kids strive to be part of the "in" crowd, they celebrate mimicking. Before that, attempts at mimicking are bullied and condemned. Why, then, do some kids get bullied for following along when others are celebrated for it?

You need a connection to people, and people need a connection to you. I want to encourage you to celebrate mimicking and flattery within your children and their friends. I stepped in one time and made a point to explain this to my children. There is no longer any condemnation in my house when an older child is upset that a younger sibling is "copying" him. Thankfully, it did put an immediate end to the behavior.

Practice "copying" others who influence you. Who do you want to become, or who do you want to emulate? That is what children do, and that is how they learn to become adults. Your kids are emulating, another word for mimicking, and you get to emulate the people you look up to as well. Who is watching and emulating you? Those are the people you are influencing. What kind of impact do you want to make on them, and where do you want to make that impact?

Impact on Society

When you discover your "why," your purpose on this earth will become clear, and momentum will propel you toward significance. A life of significance starts from putting others first in your thinking and actions. You will become an influencer of influencers and leave a lasting impact on society. Influence takes time. It is not the passage of time that gives you significant influence, but the time of positioning yourself to lead through your gifts, strengths, and heart creating value to others.

People who live extremely abundant, successful lives got there because their focus was on the value they could provide to others. It was never about themselves or about becoming rich. Most people who achieve greatness and success got there from following their passion, becoming a master at their gift or trade, and serving a big need.

Eventually, those steps from a person's passion lead to financial benefits or wealth. Before financial wealth arrives, you will experience fullness and abundance in other areas of your life through following your passion and knowing your strengths and gifts. You will achieve greatness and joy in your life in intellectual, spiritual, relational, and possibly physical areas. When your life is full of joy and happiness, and you are doing what you are designed to do, society will feel your impact.

It takes mastery of yourself first. When you master yourself, you will begin to learn the art of enabling others to master themselves. As your skills improve in enabling others to grow alongside you, your social impact, strength, and influence will be felt by those around you. You will be attractive to the people around you because they will want to be more like you. Your presence and calming power appeal to those who still need to grow into it. Your ability to create affinity and influence with the influencers you surround yourself with will have a ripple effect through the world. You get to decide how far your impact will reach based on your willingness to grow, learn, and get involved.

Oprah Winfrey is a great example of growth in mastering self. She was open to learning, receiving feedback, and accepting mistakes. Eventually, Oprah became the person to listen and look up to for advice and guidance. Do you recall Oprah's Favorite Things and her willingness to give away gifts to the audience? *The Oprah Winfrey Show* was an opportunity to enable others to grow themselves, to learn new things, and eventually, the world started to notice what she was doing.

Oprah is a marvel, and she is a normal ordinary person just like the rest of us. She builds orphanages and schools and spreads good all over the world. It's doubtful many people who knew Oprah early in her life thought she would grow up to be a voice to people across the globe. It's possible to be whomever and whatever you choose to become. You have the same opportunity as everyone else on this planet.

<u>The Keys to Living a Significant Life</u>

- **Action is imperative:** Being agreeable and passive feels safe because nothing can go wrong, you won't make anyone mad, and you will rarely get in trouble. You won't fail when you play it safe by waiting around and following the group. However, you also won't experience your successes and pursue your true purpose.
- **Lift up the people around you:** Studies prove that we learn and grow exponentially when teaching someone else.
- **Respond with empathy and attunement:** Attunement is relaying your understanding of what someone else is going through and what the person is feeling without giving advice, fixing, helping, or dismissing what is being said.

- **Put others first:** When your focus is outward, it makes your challenges and worries seem smaller and less insignificant.
- **Give back to your community:** Science has proven that people who donate both time and money to charities will personally experience greater joy and happiness and will live longer.
- **Lead a cause you are passionate about:** Take a stand for something you feel strongly about improving. You can start small. Learn and practice by getting on board or helping with someone's mission. Helping other people fight for their cause will foster a deep understanding of what works well and bring better compassion and understanding toward the people who offer to help you.

Going to work at your job for enough money to buy food, clothing, and shelter is not your why or your purpose. One of my mentors calls this your platform. Simon Sinek says to start with "why." Whatever you are passionate about standing up for is the reason you get up in the morning to work. It's your "WHY."

I'm not sure whose quote this is, but it is the core of impact and influence:

> *Be willing to be known as somebody who stands for something, and you will never be forgotten.*

Until I was in my forties, I spent most of my life afraid to talk to people. I did not speak well in groups, and I was hesitant to speak up for myself. I especially did not want people looking at me when I spoke, and I was anxious and stressed when I was the center of attention. Obviously, becoming a person of influence or impact was not very likely for me, even though it was what I felt called to do. Recently, I found a piece of paper dated July 17, 2005. It was in a giant filing cabinet and printed in the most beautiful blue font:

My drive is to be an Influencer.
I want to make a difference in the world
and I want my children to grow up
knowing their mom is someone who
does great things for other people.
The best way to influence the world
is through wealth and a giving spirit.

God does not call the qualified. He qualifies the called. Who are you meant to be in this world? What are you called to do? Whatever you are meant to be is up to you. I want to encourage you to pursue your passions and your purpose. You were meant to thrive.

14

Live Your Life of Abundance

Do nothing out of selfish ambition or vain conceit.
Rather, in humility value others above yourselves,
not looking to your own interests but the interests of others.
(Philippians 2:3–4 NIV)

LIVING YOUR LIFE of abundance is about learning to thrive. You were not meant to live on this earth to merely survive. You were not put here to merely breathe, use up resources, and die. Your life has a plan. It has a purpose, and you have a purpose for being here. Living your life of abundance requires you to have a great relationship with the tool of money to grow into the person you are supposed to become. Money is necessary to live on this planet, and you will need financial resources to do great things in this world.

My earnest desire is that you experience an enthusiasm to learn more about these topics and transform your life into one of thriving. Along with that, I hope you grow your capacity to retain financial blessings in your life and learn how to enhance and retain what you are earning through the strategies introduced in this book. Your rejuvenated enthusiasm will make a difference for those around you.

For myself, I got tired of living merely to survive. Abundance is thriving, and it encapsulates every area of your life. Abundance is love, joy, peace, happiness, health, passion, focus, purpose, excellence, blessing, friendship, freedom of choice, and financial resources. Having abundance in your life is about living the full, rich life you deserve, the blessings and life that your family deserves.

Abundance is your freedom to choose. It's about deciding for yourself what you want and not feeling stuck. Freedom is about having hope and a drive to do what is in your heart to live your deepest desires. I earnestly desire for you to live a life of thriving. I want you to experience your life to the fullest. I yearn for you to live your life of abundance.

When you experience abundance in your life, it multiplies, and you share it with the people around you. Your blessings, happiness, joy, passion, and love will create more opportunities for people in your sphere of influence to experience greater levels of abundance as well. The people around you who are affected positively will create an even larger circle of influence and abundance.

Don't give anyone the power to knock you off track. You get to decide what you want in life. You are in control of your future and your destiny. The time and money you invest in yourself are the effort and choices that give you the highest return on investment. Working on your mindset and emotional intelligence will yield big returns. These will provide you with an orientation toward growth. Investing in yourself allows you to be forward-thinking, to make room for curiosity, and to be open to learning new skills. Take every opportunity to ask for feedback to make changes that improve what you are doing. Strive to retain control of your self-care to be the best version of yourself.

Live, More than Enough

People who live in abundance recognize that they don't know everything and don't attempt to do all that is required by themselves. When you are open to learning, you will find that you can learn something from every person. There is always more to learn, and another person may see it from a different angle or understanding. Sometimes people act as if they already know everything on a topic. It can be a learned behavior the way I learned from my upbringing. Other people who respond that way may be acting from fear, or they need to work on their emotional intelligence to make room for that change in their lives.

Abundance is an internal belief that gives you direction on living and existing in the world.

Money is one of the tools you have available to achieve what you need. You can choose to use the tool you have within your reach, such as a hammer to build a garden box for your neighbor or to fix something for your grandmother. You can also choose to use the tool in your reach, a hammer, to swing at someone's head and injure or kill them. It is not the hammer's fault that you hurt someone with the simple tool in your hand. You can choose to do good with the tool, or you can do bad. It is always your choice.

When you embrace a life of abundance, you have chosen to live your life from the viewpoint of autonomy. Autonomy is knowing that you have choices, and you believe that you can attain whatever you dream up or desire. Living your life of abundance is about living your version of freedom, that whatever is for you. Certainly, it is easier to attain financial freedom when replacing less income and living a simplified life. It is also true that it can be easier to acquire more assets that produce cash flow when a person has much higher discretionary income.

Both are true.
And you can have anything you desire.

The question that shifted my thinking to foster answers that brought a deeper belief around abundance is:

How can I retain what I currently have and enhance what I'm already doing?

This question has brought a powerful shift in my life for friends, family members, and the people I mentor because it always makes people pause. It's not a question anyone had asked me previously, and anyone who hears it seems to pause and ponder the question a moment. The pondering is because your brain has not previously encountered an opportunity to answer that question. Once you ask it of yourself, your brain will begin to work on an answer. As your brain begins to formulate new neural pathways for this question, it will become capable of generating solutions to that question more and more rapidly every time you ask it. Keep asking yourself and allow others to hear the question. You are beginning to formulate new ways of thinking and being.

How can I get both? When your brain starts looking for answers to that question, it will guide your thinking and decision-making to a solution that encompasses both/and. It's similar to a toddler who wants everything he wants and has no intention to give up until he gets both. You are retraining your brain to learn how to have *both,* such as your cash and your investment or your time and your travel.

You can retrain your brain to think thoughts of abundance in all areas of your life. Stop choosing to limit yourself the way your parents and most of your life experiences may have trained you to think. You no longer need to choose one or the other. You can choose "both/and." Your goal can be to continually move toward an abundance way of thinking and to have both of anything you want in life. You can have this *and* that. In your finances, you can keep "both" your current resources "and" enhance and acquire more of what you need to live your life of freedom and abundance. True wealth and abundance are created by thinking outside the box with nontraditional ideas.

Use this book as a reference as you continue to change and evolve your mindset and grow in viewing the world with an abundance mindset. As your abundance mindset grows, it will increase your capacity to earn and retain more financial resources. When

I first started learning how wealthy people think about money, I could not have understood most of the topics covered in this book. You will want to start at the simplest concepts and review the information as your capacity grows.

There was a audiobook that I listened to many times between five and seven years ago. After hearing the same chapter around ten times, it occurred to me that I wasn't yet capable of understanding the material. Repetition of material that did not make sense wasn't helping me learn the information. It became more important that I develop my base of knowledge to understand the material in the book. It didn't matter how many times I heard the information until my skills, ability, and understanding had increased.

Recently, it became evident that I should listen to the entire book again. My first thought was, "No way; I've spent enough hours of my life listening to that book." Then I realized my ability to use the information had drastically increased. Much of the information here is something you have never heard previously. You will experience the same phenomenon with the information in this book. Some of it will be relevant to where you are now, and some of it might as well be in a different language. It is not a reflection on you. It's a natural tendency in learning new concepts.

It is also a great practice to research the concepts on your own and look at other information on these topics. You will find a whole world of information. In the next chapter is a list of books that have greatly impacted me. They have facilitated my transformation and enhanced my ability to understand these concepts. I hope you will experience a yearning to learn more and grow toward freedom for yourself and the people you love.

Freedom on YOUR Terms

A friend and I started a mastermind group. It has evolved quite a bit since it began pre-COVID. I intend to keep growing and expanding on the content, growth, and transformation that people are experiencing. It's called Freedom—On YOUR Terms, and we recently had an engaging conversation around a case study with the question how each of us would choose in different real-life scenarios. As you might guess, everyone had a different perspective and spin on how someone could best proceed. The time did not end with a consensus. However, we each learned a lot and were able to see the viewpoints of each other. It was one of the most fun topics we have had in the group.

Our place as leaders and freedom seekers is to listen to all opinions and understand all viewpoints. Why would they do it that way? Is there another option that will give the same or better results? What is the best strategy for me? How can I enhance what I'm doing with that new idea?

After reading this book, you will begin to develop thoughts and ideas about how you can have both/and in your life and your finances. It doesn't always work that you get everything you want. But the important thing is that you will get much closer to having exactly what you want when that is your primary objective.

Beginning with the objective of having both will allow you to think through to the end. Subsequently, the results will be to work backward and negotiate with others for an option that works for all involved. You will have the opportunity to negotiate a win/win solution that offers the best solution, as close to both/ and that you can get.

Everyone has a different place of comfort in one's finances. Beginning your journey can bring an opportunity for your place of safety to be stretched. Sometimes that can be uncomfortable, and you want to notice and respect what gives you the most peace. I prefer having high cash reserves and a high minimum account balance in all checking accounts. That gives me the security to ensure that all debt payments and expenses are paid without worry. I had to push the envelope and do it differently to learn what offered me the most peace. Others prefer to use a lower loan to value to offset risk and maintain stability in their lives. Everyone has a different formula to create abundance and mitigate risk. Honor what works best for you and account for that in your planning.

Notice when you are experiencing stress. Talk through the scenario with your spouse, business partner, or someone else that you trust. It may give you a great perspective to talk it out, or your friend may notice something that you don't realize. One thing that causes excessive stress for me is managing finances that are constantly running close to zero. I recently experienced stress when one of our new investment purchases incurred higher vacancy and greater rehab expenses immediately after taking ownership than we had originally forecast. After talking about it several times and feeling like a complainer, I finally realized why I was so stressed. Now I have learned to speak my preference upfront and refuse to ignore my reserve plan the way I compromised my values on this purchase. Maintaining high reserves is my peace of mind, and it allows me the opportunity to continue living in a place of abundance. You are the only one who can know your area of comfort and honor that for yourself.

<u>The Importance of Real Estate</u>

After understanding the traditional financial market, I began to wonder about a very important question: How is it that wealthy people got wealthy in the first place, and more importantly, how did they stay wealthy? It became clear that real estate is generally included in every wealthy person's portfolio. There must be a reason for that. I began to learn and explore investing in real estate as well.

There are four clear-cut reasons why real estate is, in some capacity, part of most large portfolios. It's because real estate has several distinct advantages to wealth enhancement and performs as a multiplier effect to any wealth retention and enhancement strategy.

In my experience, it is beneficial for everyone to understand why real estate makes such a difference to your strategy and the reasons why owning real estate can multiply your efforts. It doesn't matter if you want to be a landlord or want nothing to do with it. It doesn't matter if you prefer to own a few properties or many. It doesn't matter if you earn more than the phase-out passive income limit. Any real estate owned will amplify your wealth retention and enhancement strategies when you understand these four sneaky benefits to real estate.

These four benefits to real estate create a get-rich-slow phenomenon. It can be easy to miss the big picture results when focused on day-to-day activities. It can be extremely difficult to notice the benefits when you don't understand where your investment gains the most advantage.

So what exactly is the big deal with real estate?

Four Real Estate Amplifiers

Leverage: The first way real estate accelerates your freedom and abundance goals is through leverage. When you use bank financing, you can buy more assets than you could independently. If it takes twenty percent of your own money to own and control the asset, your value enhancement is much greater than purchasing an asset without any financing.

Depreciation: The second multiplying benefit of real estate is the tax benefits or depreciation of the asset. You get to depreciate your ownership and deduct part of the asset while holding it. Many specific IRS rules go along with real estate and depreciation, so you will want to consult a good real estate CPA about your particular situation.

Appreciation: The third pillar that amplifies real estate as an investment strategy is the asset's appreciation. As long as you maintain your property, appreciation typically is similar or matches inflation. That means the value of your asset will stay relative even with the cost of living in your society.

Cash Flow: The fourth and the most valuable benefit to real estate is cash flow. The cash flow pays for the asset and leaves raising cash for you. You can calculate cash flow for each property after all expenses, including taxes and insurance, have been paid. When you use leverage to purchase an asset, the cash flow is often not a large number per month. As you pay down debt, the asset value will increase, and additional rent will increase cash flow.

Cash flow comes from renting or leasing your asset to someone to use during your period of ownership. There are several advantages to cash flow. The first is that someone else pays your mortgage and expenses to own the asset. Next, you can have cash flow that produces more for you to keep as profit. The last and most important advantage in cash flow is that rental costs will keep up with inflation.

Sometimes owners do not raise rents because they feel bad about charging more. There is very little benefit to society by charging less than market rent to your tenants. The typical person will spend all the money they bring into their household, and housing is the biggest expense in everyone's budget. You are doing a disservice to your tenants by charging too little in rent because they will spend that money on something. It is more valuable for you to enjoy ownership and have resources available to make necessary repairs and upkeep on the property. Your tenants will spend all the discretionary money in their budget, so you might as well charge them what you need to take care of the property best.

Contrary to many real estate investors, I am not against having traditional retirement accounts. We have "both" traditional retirement accounts "and" real estate in our portfolio. When you live your life of abundance, you will realize how important it is to take advantage of all opportunities that present themselves. You have the freedom to choose for yourself. You have the freedom to pick which investments work for you and when you want to participate. You also get to change them whenever it's best. Don't feel obligated to fit into anyone's mold.

Owning or investing in real estate can be done more ways than we could cover in this book. You get to research if it's best for you and how it works best for your goals and family. If you want to live your life of abundance and if you want the freedom to live the life you want to live, real estate will amplify and enhance every step you are taking. It is best to get a coach or mentor to avoid many real estate pitfalls. That will also help you to enhance and retain your resources.

Live Your Life of Abundance

Abundance is when your core state of existing and underlying belief system operate around knowing that more than enough of any resource is available to supply your and everyone else's needs. Abundance is not wealth, and wealth is not simply about money. You live your life of abundance when you live with the underlying belief that more than enough is available for you, and you get to choose anything you want in your life.

You live in abundance when you know that you are in control of your life's desires, and you can acquire anything you need without taking anything away from someone else. Your mindset, values, and underlying belief system will dictate how you view the world and what is most important for you. If you want everything that I've laid out in this book, you will need to put in the hard work to get it.

Many of you will find, as I did, that your upbringing, family of origin, and life experiences did not prepare you with the capacity to get all that you want in life. I was not fully capable of living my life of abundance, even with much help from trustworthy and safe people who had gone before me. You will need people who have conquered their limitations and learned how to live a life of abundance in ways you haven't yet.

You may be like me and know that you want more for yourself but not know exactly where to go next or how to get it. ***Something in my heart said, "I am meant for more."*** Instead of setting out to achieve what was in my heart, I spent years of my life wandering aimlessly and stepping back into the same struggles that I had been in before.

Reading or listening to this book will make a difference in your life. Doing the assignments, journaling your thoughts, and documenting your transformation will give you tremendous results. Finding trusted people, asking for help when you need it, and searching for answers will provide you with traction to achieve whatever is in your heart.

We started a nonprofit to help well-intended wanderers, like ourselves, conquer limitations and move past the things holding them back. Our nonprofit is named GRASP because we know that anything you want is within your grasp. All you need to do is reach out and get it. Our mission is to empower you to pursue your passions and purpose. We want to connect you to the tools and resources you need to achieve it. By connecting to the right people and trusting the right resources, you can achieve anything. You can look us up on Facebook, Instagram, YouTube, or our website, or you may reach me directly by email at grasp. gives@gmail.com.

> *Our mission is to empower you to pursue your passions and purpose and connect you with the tools and resources you need to achieve it.*

If you need help or have questions, we will assist you. I want you to succeed. I want you to feel in control of your life and your financial future. I want you to live your life of abundance. Everything you want is available to you. You get to choose what you want in your life. You have the power to get it. You can live your life of abundance and decide to thrive.

GRASP

We encourage you to bring your dreams into existence, live your life with passion, find your purpose, and build relationships that matter.

It's WITHIN YOUR GRASP.

My Most Impactful Reads

Secrets of the Millionaire Mind by T. Harv Eker

Rich Dad Poor Dad by Robert Kiyosaki

The Power of the Other by Dr. Henry Cloud

Favor the Road to Success by Bob Buess

The One Minute Millionaire
by Mark Victor Hansen and Robert G. Allen

What Is Prosperity and Does God Want You to Have It?
By Walter Hallam

Mind Power into the 21st Century by John Kehoe

What to Say When You Talk to Yourself by Shad Helmstetter

Beyond Positive Thinking by Dr. Robert Anthony

The Lifestyle Investor by Justin Donald

Grit by Angela Duckworth

The Like Switch by Jack Schafer

About the Author

MARGO SPILDE RESIDES in Springfield, Missouri, with her husband, three children, one spoiled dog, and one lop-eared rabbit. She is a Christ-follower, wife, mom, friend, finance enthusiast, real estate investor, promoter of good in the world, Rotarian, entrepreneur, Freedom coach, and author. Some of her favorite pastimes include spending time with her family, traveling, water skiing, hiking, and talking money, real estate, or human behavior with anyone who will engage. She loves life and wants everyone to live a life filled with joy and passion.

Margo's purpose is to equip others to do what God has called them to do. She has a passion for sharing what she has learned and encouraging others to follow their purpose and live their lives with passion and joy.

When you change your thinking from scarcity to abundance, your current reality will change to abundance also. Through Margo's quest to find that "thing" that she is destined to do, she hopes to share what she's learned and inspire others to live a life of abundance. **Do more, Be more, Achieve more**.

**Be joyful always;
pray continually;
give thanks in all circumstances,
for this is God's will for you
in Christ Jesus.
(1 Thessalonians 5:16–18 NIV)**

Bibliography

"Bruce Tainio" (n.d.). Retrieved from Wave Quantum Blog: https://wavequantumblog.uk/2021/02/03/bruce-tainio/

"Eight Levels of Charity" (n.d.). Retrieved from chabad.org: https://www.chabad.org/library/article_cdo/aid/45907/jewish/Eight-Levels-of-Charity.htm

"Gift of the Heart—Giving in Buddhism" (n.d.). Retrieved from UrbanDharma.org: https://www.urbandharma.org/udharma8/gift.html#:~:text=Buddhism%20teaches%20that%20we%20exist%20in%20a%20vast,the%20tradi-tional%20view%20and%20the%20exhortation%20to%20practice.

"Largest Religions in the World" (n.d.). Retrieved from World Atlas. com: https://www.worldatlas.com/articles/largest-religions-in-the-world.html

"Latter Day Saints" (n.d.). Retrieved from Religion News Service: https://religionnews.com/2019/12/03/i-just-paid-my-mormon-tithing-why-dont-i-feel-better-about-it/#:~:text=Research%20on%20generosity%20shows%20that%20Mormons%20are%20famous,at%20least%2010%25%20of%20their%20income%20to%20charity.

"Mormon Tithing" (n.d.). Retrieved from Mormonwiki.com: https://www.mormonwiki.com/Mormon_Tithing

"Pluralism Files: The Five Pillars" (n.d.). Retrieved from Harvard. edu: https://hwpi.harvard.edu/files/pluralism/files/the_five_pillars_1.pdf

"Royal Raymond Rife" (n.d.). Retrieved from Wave Quantum Blog: https://wavequantumblog.uk/2021/01/31/dr-royal-raymond-rife/

"Science of Generosity" (n.d.). Retrieved from https://generosityresearch.nd.edu/

"Traditions of Giving in Hinduism" (n.d.). Retrieved from Alliance Magazine: https://www.alliancemagazine.org/feature/traditions-of-giving-in-hinduism/

P. Weipking and R. Bekkers (2010). "A literature review of empirical studies of philanthropy: eight mechanisms that drive charitable giving." *Nonprofit and Voluntary Sector Quarterly.*

"Word/Philanthropy" (n.d.). Retrieved from Etymoline.com: https://www.etymonline.com/word/philanthropy

CPSIA information can be obtained
at www.ICGtesting.com
Printed in the USA
LVHW050756050522
717591LV00002B/12